Growing
Dahlias

CROOM HELM LONDON

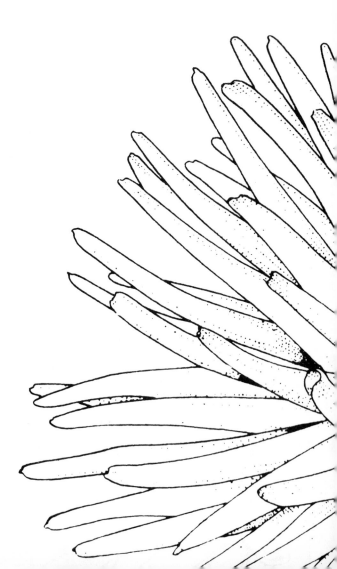

PHILIP DAMP

Growing
Dahlias

© 1981 Philip Damp
Croom Helm Ltd, 2-10 St John's Road, London SW11

British Library Cataloguing in Publication Data

Damp, Philip
    Growing Dahlias.
    1. Dahlias.
    I. Title
    635.9'33'55   SB413.D13
    ISBN 0-7099-0800-8

Jacket illustration shows 'Real Delight' (Front panel)
and 'Nationwide' (back panel).
Line Drawings by Sue Sharples

Published in North America

by:

Timber Press
P.O. Box 1632
Beaverton, Oregon 97075

Typeset by Columns.
Printed in Great Britain by Redwood Burn, Trowbridge,
and Bound by Leighton Straker, London

Contents

List of Figures

Introduction

It is almost 200 years since the dahlia arrived in Britain from Mexico after a brief stopover in Spain. But it is only in recent years that this flamboyant species can be said to have truly made its mark and to have become one of our most popular summer flowers. There are probably very good social, even political, as well as horticultural reasons for this, as the growing interest of the ordinary citizen in gardening and the pleasures that it can bring must obviously stem from the acquisition of space in which to grow anything at all.

In the early part of this century, gardening was still something to be enjoyed only by the rich, and if the man in the street had any space at all, then it was devoted to the growing of foodstuffs rather than ornamentals. There is ample evidence for this in the history of the National Dahlia Society, which celebrates its centenary in 1981.

For 50 years, the membership of this august body languished, as the major part of its interest was devoted to the cultivation of the dahlia for exhibition. A spark of hope did light up the thirties, but even in the immediate post-war years the total number of members did not exceed 800, but that was to be the rock upon which a virtual revolution was founded, and as home ownership, and with it gardening space, continued to spread throughout the British Isles, so did an interest in the dahlia that wildly exceeded the dreams of the early pioneers. By the mid-sixties, that 800 had risen dramatically to a figure in excess of 7,000, and while the last 20 years has seen a levelling out of this to a more conservative 4,000, there is no doubt that the dahlia had become so popular that its future was permanently assured.

It would be unfair to attribute the rise in interest entirely to the new army of homeowners, as the dahlia played no small part in the escalation itself. Gardeners, new or old, soon discovered for themselves how easily they could grow the flower which was so adaptable, that it could be used for almost any purpose — bedding out during the summer at very low cost, raising a mass of blooms for cutting for the home or for friends and, of course, grown with extra skill for exhibition. Handled with care, there was also the very important fact that the dahlia could be economic, for not only did the tubers provide a cost-free supply of plant material for each succeeding summer, but offered the chance of surpluses which could be given to friends or even exchanged for other horticultural things.

Accompanying this widespread popularity was yet another army, the professionals. They sparked off an international supply and demand situation that persists to the present day. British dahlia nurserymen with their long established skills and business acumen, and with traditions that spread back, in many cases, to the last century, were quick to realise the potential of the dahlia and its large market, and so too did the continental suppliers. Prominent among this group were the Dutch, who through their trade organisation the Netherlands Dahlia Society, founded just after World War 1, and via the individual specialists who catered for the needs of the truly enthusiastic, an avalanche of new dahlias in different colours and even different forms was available to the new dahlia lovers. It was not unusual for several hundred novelties to be released each autumn, and in addition to this wide choice provided by the European trade, new dahlias were reaching Britain from America, Australia, New Zealand, South Africa and Japan, where there was a similar upsurge in interest. That interchange is still taking place to the benefit of everyone who loves this flower, and in Holland the cultivation and export of dahlia roots has reached such proportions, that it is a vital part of her foreign trade, with some 50 million tubers sold overseas in 1980!

It was not possible, of course, that such a transformation could take place in the world of gardens and gardeners without many other benefits. As most will testify who have grown and become involved in the many facets of dahlia hobbying, there is a golden thread of friendship that winds itself inextricably through the whole pattern of things. It is nowhere more apparent than within the massive network of horticultural societies that cover the British Isles, and in a genuine hands-across-the-sea involvement with other similar societies in the four corners of the world. The National Dahlia Society has over 1,000 affiliated bodies and it would be impossible to visit any one of the Society's flower shows each summer and not see how the abundance of this flower enhances the event and intrigues the visitors.

Among fellow enthusiasts, individual friendships are made and group friendships flourish. Awards are exchanged annually between groups and even between enthusiast and enthusiast, and stock is exchanged world wide and this can only contribute to a better understanding of each other and the ways in which we all live.

In this book I have endeavoured to outline the pleasures that can be obtained from growing dahlias. It will be quickly appreciated that the dahlia is easy to grow and grow well, and I trust that in these chapters there is enough evidence to convince even the beginner that he or she can produce blooms of such quality that not only the practical needs of garden decoration are satisfied, but also the obvious satisfaction of personal achievement are enjoyed. Some may well find this joy in the creation of a garden filled with a kaleidoscope of colour from July to the frosts of autumn; others in the production of a host of elegantly formed dahlias that can grace the home or be cut for the delight of friends. And there will be some, I trust, who may enter into the rarer pleasures of exhibition culture, which invokes in those who practise this particular aspect of dahlia growing, a will and persistence to do better with each succeeding season, and which carries with it a special reward — that of comradeship and a feeling of belonging.

I have enjoyed the pleasures that the dahlia can offer for 30 years. The last 14 of these have been spent as fulltime General Secretary of the National Dahlia Society and as dahlia correspondent of many gardening magazines and papers, including *Garden News*, for whom I have worked for over 20 years. It has meant that dahlias have been my life, and there is not a moment to regret in all of those three decades.

In this introduction, however, it would be unfair of me to dwell upon my own rewards from my long association with the dahlia but rather to pay tribute to the many who have helped me. To my wife Liz, this book is dedicated. Without her assistance and co-operation none of it would have been possible. Her forbearance and patience are beyond price, and that she continues to be as helpful and cheerful as she was when I first brought the dahlia into our lives never fails to amaze me!

To my many friends in the world of amateur and professional dahlia culture, sincere thanks are also extended. Their assistance over the years has been of inestimable value, and if this book helps others to appreciate the hobby, as my friends and I have for so long, then I would wish my colleagues to know that a great deal of the knowledge imparted in these pages has rubbed off on me from them.

All of them, without exception, I am sure, would join me in extending an invitation to join us in our very special world. All flowers are beautiful, and all give the grower or admirer particular pleasure. In the dahlia world we have all of this and yet something more — can we persuade you to come and join with us?

Philip Damp

CHAPTER 1

History and Evolution

The history of the dahlia, to say the very least, is an exciting and romantic story. It has links with the courts of Spain and the dahlia's eventual arrival in Europe from Mexico was to spark off argument and dissent amongst many of the leading horticulturists of the day. The dahlia grows wild in Colombia and Guatemala as well as Mexico, but the original species of our garden dahlia – *D. variabilis* – came from Mexico.

The very first dahlias were discovered by botanists accompanying the Spanish Conquistadores, who found that the Aztec Indians in Mexico called the flower *accotli*, which literally translated means 'hollow pipe'. Indeed this description of the dahlia was apt, because there were species of gigantic proportions, towering 30 ft or more in height, and others that even enmeshed themselves with trees and which had hollow stems that the natives used for carrying water over long distances in a viaduct-like system. The dahlia was first noted by these early botanists in the sixteenth century, but it was to be another 200 years before specimens were to arrive in Europe. In that intervening age, the dahlia had become a garden plant of the Spanish colonists, and it is believed that the first arrivals, named as *D. pinnata*, *D. rosea* and *D. coccinea* came from this source.

That the dahlia was a natural hybrid was beyond argument, and when these first samples arrived at the Royal Gardens, Madrid in 1789 the curator, a certain Abbé Cavanilles, flowered them successfully and described

13

them in detail in a book he produced called *Icones*. In all this work, the pioneer Cavanilles was assisted by a Swedish botanist named Andreas Dahl, a former pupil of Linnaeus (famous for his creation of the international language of flowers). It was to honour Dahl that the generous Abbot eventually designated this new arrival as the *Dahlia*, although later others were to offer a different name.

From Madrid, roots and seeds of the newcomer were sent all over Europe. In Paris, at Le Jardin des Plantes, they were tried for purposes other than garden enhancement, and in the early part of the nineteenth century they were sold in French markets for food. It is recorded that this Mexican plant was not to the liking of continental palates, and the roots were used for animal feed, although even this practice ceased very quickly. England also experimented with this bizarre use of the new arrival, and dahlia tubers were sold as 'Jerusalem Artichokes' in London markets, but were soon discarded when it was found that they were tasteless.

Meanwhile specimens of the dahlia had found their way to Russia, and were grown by a Professor Georgi, and named Georgina in his honour. There is a contradictory story that the dahlia's name was changed to *Georgina* in honour of our own George III, but the Russian version is probably the true one. It took a long time before the horticulturists of Europe eventually agreed on Dahlia, Cavanilles's original name for the species, and even today in some of the remoter parts of Russia this flower is still referred to as Georgina.

The arrival of the dahlia in Britain was to spark off a floral furore, unparalleled in horticultural history. The first seeds and plants imported just before the turn of the eighteenth century were lost, either from insufficient knowledge or carelessness. Later imports, starting with those credited to Lady Holland in 1804, which came from the original plants sent to Cavanilles from Mexico, were successfully flowered, and other samples sent by an Alexander von Humboldt direct from Mexico produced seedlings in many hues and form variations. The early experimenters needed no further proof, and horticulturists of the time were quick to realise that here was a flower with a future. And what a future! By the 1830s hundreds of new varieties were catalogued, a number that was to escalate into thousands over the next 30 years. Dominating this early scene in Britain was the form that apparently intrigued everyone. It was a fully double, globular form that was named as the globe form, later the famous Double Show and Fancy type, which today we know as the Ball Dahlia.

Dahlia societies sprang up all over Britain, and challenge shows between the gentry, who constituted their membership, followed. The dahlia had arrived as a flower of fascination with the ability to change its face, colour and form almost at the drop of a hat.

High prices were paid for novelties that, in the eyes of the purchaser, were different. Two hundred pounds or more, a small fortune in those days, was paid for new seedlings of the famous Double Show and Fancy type, and an asking price of 100 guineas was not unusual for many seedlings. By the middle of the nineteenth century, the varieties on offer numbered thousands, almost all with the now familiar globular form. Changes, however, were imminent, and in Germany a miniaturised form of the Double Show arrived. The form was the same as the larger types, but neater and more compact. The Germans named the new arrival Lilliput (for obvious reasons) and this type is well known today by most gardeners as the Pompon.

Single variations were also coming to the fore, and the collerette type — a single-centred bloom with a secondary row of petals (the collar — hence the name) was discovered in France; and from Holland the very first cactus form emerged with the arrival of the spiky-petalled variety which was named *D. Juarezii*. The latter, named after a Mexican president of the time, has often been credited to Mexican hybridists, but the Dutch story is well substantiated, and is accepted as the correct one by dahlia enthusiasts world wide. The *Juarezii* breakthrough was, perhaps, the most important of the dahlia's changes, as it was the original ancestor of all our modern cactus and semi-cactus varieties, as well as many of the decorative

15

formations that we have in commercial production today.

With the arrival of the cactus formations that were spawned in profusion in the latter half of the nineteenth century, came a lessening of the interest in the Double Show and Fancy. They were still popular, of course, but the cactus forms offered other channels to explore and a different set of values for the shows and exhibitions that were the delight of the Victorians; but there was one great problem. The new form was difficult to stage; stems were weak and exhibitors had to display their wares on boards. Seeking for blooms that would hold themselves erect in a vase or clear of the foliage in the garden gave rise to experiments with another form — that which resembles the peony.

The broader, semi-double petalling of the peony type, examples of which are still in cultivation today, came from the continent, and was possessed of reasonably strong stems — something the hybridists had been looking for. From the peony it was a short step to the flat-petalled, fully double form of the decorative dahlia that we know today, and whilst it did take a long time for this new form to become popular, there is no doubt that the modern fascination with the decorative form, the cactus and semi-cactus forms owes a lot to the marriage between *Juarezii* and the peony.

In this brief history of the dahlia, it is obvious that it was the horticulturists of the western world who had changed the dahlia. For untold centuries it had remained as a wild, natural hybrid. With a few strokes from a camel-hair brush the commercial world of the nineteenth century had transformed this flower into something that would be unrecognisable in its country of origin. From those early samples sent to Cavanilles in Madrid, has come a range of varieties, form and colour that offers something to delight and intrigue the most fastidious gardener. A new flower or the changed version of it, however, needed more than its colourful face to excite worldwide interest.

In 1881 the National Dahlia Society was formed to cater for the needs of those who had been intrigued with this new arrival. Chiefly, this need was for the provision of exhibitions or shows where the talents of the grower could be pitted against those of his friends or contemporaries. Shows where the dahlia held sway had begun in the 1830s, and continued for half a century or more without an organising body. With the arrival of the NDS this was to change, and whilst the first officers and committee seemed obsessed with the spirit of competition, later aims and expressed policies of this august body were to exploit the dahlia as something that could and would bring pleasure and colour into the lives of ordinary gardeners. Today that object has been achieved, and the century-old National Dahlia Society presides over a dahlia scene which covers the entire world. Societies, both national and local, exist in their thousands, and the interchange of information and stock continues apace with the NDS, the world's largest society, leading the way.

I often wonder what the modest Abbé Cavanilles might have thought could he visit the world's largest dahlia show, organised by the National Dahlia Society and held in the Royal Horticultural Halls, London, every September. Or what his comment would have been should he walk around the world's leading dahlia trials, held every summer in the RHS Gardens, Wisley, Surrey. That such beauty should have emanated from those few wizened tubers and seeds he had received from a country he had never seen, perhaps, would have merited the term miracle. A word not unknown to our ancestors and which, in the case of the dahlia, bears a close resemblance to the truth.

CHAPTER 2

Dahlia Forms and Types

It is not inappropriate that a chapter on the varying forms and types of the modern dahlia should follow immediately a chapter dealing with the origins and history of this flower, which showed that the dahlia had a startling beginning, with the discovery that it was ready to change its form, the colour of its petals, and even the height, formation and substance of its foliage within just one year's seedling span. Perhaps it is this element of surprise and anticipation that attracts so many gardeners to grow and adore the flower.

One of the most difficult tasks that administrators of the dahlia have encountered in the century or more since classification and cataloguing of it began, has been to reach an agreement on descriptions or names for the many types that have emerged. Fifteen years ago the Royal Horticultural Society was given the task of bringing together the work of those early years into some semblance of order, and it produced its *Tentative Classified List and International Register of Dahlia Names* in 1969, which has remained one of the dahlia aficionado's classical reference books ever since, and contains some 20,000 variety descriptions, ranging from form, colour, raiser's name and country to the introducer, usually a trader. This task, commissioned by the International Horticultural Congress held at Brussels and in Maryland (USA) in the sixties, created the International Registration Authority for Dahlia Names, and that office still remains with the Royal Horticultural Society.

The register combines the accumulated talents and work of dahlia societies and professional bodies world wide, and in an attempt to bring some form of order to a previously confused situation, national organisations were asked to relinquish phraseology used, perhaps for generations, in favour of a common language of the dahlia. In this they were reasonably successful, although it is fair to comment that there has been some drift away from the original aims and intentions during the last decade, and a number of authorities have either re-introduced or retained descriptions that are not used elsewhere internationally. The main cause of this apparent anomaly has several root causes. Chiefly, however, it is basically climatic in that a dahlia of one formation growing in, say, the British climate, will differ dramatically in form and indeed size, if grown in parts of the USA or Australia. The problem of complete uniformity would appear to be an idealist's dream but it cannot be denied that the RHS in its role as Registrar has done a fine job, and its final choice of forms and titles is one that is almost universally accepted.

The Royal Society, in the three years' preparation of the Registry, eventually decided to maintain ten basic classifications as follows:

Group 1. Single-flowered Dahlias
Group 2. Anemone-flowered Dahlias
Group 3. Collerette Dahlias
Group 4. Peony-flowered Dahlias
Group 5. Decorative Dahlias
Group 6. Ball Dahlias
Group 7. Pompon Dahlias
Group 8. Cactus Dahlias
Group 9. Semi-cactus Dahlias
Group 10. Miscellaneous Dahlias

The size factor, a very different facet of classification world wide, was broken into five categories as follows:

A. Giant flowered
B. Large flowered

C. Medium flowered
D. Small flowered
E. Miniature flowered

Fifteen recognised colour variations were given:

White, Yellow, Orange, Bronze, Flame, Red, Dark Red, Light Pink, Dark Pink (includes Lavender and Mauve), Wine (includes Purple and Violet), Blend (a combination of two colours), Blends (combinations of three colours or more), Bicoloured (two distinct colours) and Variegated (multicoloured varieties).

From this basic formula for classification, a coding system was devised which identified any dahlia instantly. For example, a variety annotated 5a-LtPk is interpreted as a light pink, giant-flowered decorative, or 9c-DkR as a medium-flowered semi-cactus, dark red. This is a very simple method which is almost as compelling as Linnaeus's introduction of Latin names for all our flowers. The question of size, as briefly related above, remains the prerogative of the various international societies, as it would have been impossible to be specific about a variety that grows to 6 in. in diameter in a London garden, when the same variety in the sunshine of California would reach a bloom width of 10 in. The National Dahlia Society has followed meticulously the recommendations of the International Registry, and its groupings from 1 to 10 follow the original. Size divisions have also been adopted by the NDS to conform with the international code, and the 'domestic' sizings have been added for the British enthusiast as follows:

A. Giant-flowered — Blooms over 10 in. (254 mm) in diameter
B. Large-flowered — Usually between 8 in. (203 mm) and 10 in. (254 mm) in diameter
C. Medium-flowered — Usually between 6 in. (152 mm) and 8 in. (203 mm) in diameter
D. Small-flowered — Usually between 4 in. (102 mm) and 6 in. (152 mm) in diameter

E. Miniature-flowered — Not usually exceeding 4 in. (102 mm) in diameter

Where colour is concerned, the NDS has also followed the international recommendations, but its added analysis of what constitutes, for example, a yellow dahlia is most useful. It specifies the following for a yellow bloom: all shades of yellow including Dresden, primrose, sulphur, mimosa, straw, lemon, amber yellow, chrome yellow (light) and maize. The analyses are continued throughout the whole range, and related for practical reference to the colour charts issued by the RHS (cost approximately £9 per set from the RHS, Vincent Square, London). The National Dahlia Society's book, which is produced under the title *Classified Directory*, is updated biannually, and is sold at the very modest price of £1 per copy — for non-members too. Should you wish to enlarge your knowledge of the dahlia's complex classification, the Secretary's address is 26 Burns Road, Lillington, Leamington Spa, Warwickshire, CV32 7ER.

Of course, it is first rate to have a detailed classification and division of the dahlia into form and colour, but for the ordinary gardener intent on getting the best from his plantings, description of the individual types is essential. After all, a dahlia can be open-centred like a daisy or it can be a foot or more in diameter, with a fully double form, and a depth (distance from front to rear of each flower) that makes the largest, the giant blooms, resemble a football when fully grown. Each type, as listed above, is described below.

Single-flowered Dahlias

The single blooms, as the name would suggest, have a single outer ring of petals which surround an open centre — sometimes called a disc. There are many fine examples of this form, and the original species were, of course, simple six- or seven-petalled blooms that would belong to this group. Today the majority of seedling-raised dahlias which are grown world wide are used for bedding out, and can be seen in our public parks and other municipal gardens, blooming in profusion from July

21

until the first frosts of October.

Mostly the height of the single-flowered varieties is restricted to something related to minimum maintenance, which means that little or no support is needed and a succession of blooms is achieved by a regular removal of the dead and dying flowers. They are particularly useful for parks, as they need not be saved in the autumn when beds are cleared, as a new supply of plants can be grown from seed the next spring. This shorter type is also useful in the small garden, and contrary to popular belief, it is possible to cut the bedding singles for vasing in the home. The range of colours is extensive, running from white to deepest purples, missing out only on the elusive blue, a colour that the dahlia has yet to achieve. For the gardener who annually grows a crop of single-flowered varieties either to fit in with a bedding scheme or for cut-flower work, there is one disadvantage: colour is a matter of luck, as any seed-sown dahlia, based on the original hybrid conception, means that there is no way that the reds or the yellows, for example, can be separated out before planting and so relate to colour schemes. There are many, however, who do not find this a failing, and are content with what is given by nature. Also, of course, seed-raised dahlias, costing just a few pence for a packet, are by far the most economical method of filling your garden with a blaze of colour and useful bloom.

Anemone-flowered Dahlias

The dahlia imitates the form of many other garden subjects, so much so that it has been called the chameleon of the horticultural world. More about that interesting facet later, but with the anemone-flowered types, the blooms have one or more outer rings of generally flattened central petals surrounding a dense group of florets that are tubular. Usually these tubular petals, which give the type its name, conceal the centre of each bloom giving them an appearance of being fully double. Some of the varieties, with less compacting of the centres, could be described as semi-double. They are a rare group, with just a handful being commercially grown. The

22

National Dahlia Society lists only eleven, most of these from abroad. They are most useful for bedding, and some of the colour combinations are fascinating, with reds and pinks and pastel shades predominating. There are no blue varieties of course — but many have hues that verge on that elusive colour, in the lilacs and mauves.

Originating in France at the turn of the century, the collerette dahlia was exploited by the British trade very quickly, followed by appreciative support from Dutch hybridists. The spelling, with an *e*, and not an *a* confuses many people, but the *e* is correct, although rarely spelt that way even in some trade catalogues!

Collerette Dahlias

The type has an outer ring of petals that are flat and reasonably broad, with a ring of smaller florets (the 'collar') usually half the length of the outside petals, in the centre. This double row surrounds an open centre, or embryo seed head, that enhances the mature bloom. The effect of the central, shorter row of petals set against the back petals offers a unique form that is perfect for contrasting colours (between the two sets of petals) which is seen frequently in this type, where for example the rear florets can be yellow with the central petals a bright red. Permutations in colour abound, and some of the most colourful flowers in the whole of the dahlia's large family are to be found here. The subtle form and wide colour variations make this group perfect for most purposes. The exception, perhaps, is in bedding schemes, as most collerettes grow to a height of 3 ft or more and require some form of staking. This plant height, however, has other advantages, as the stems are firm and strong, ideal for cut-flower work. Vasing these lovely dahlias is a pleasure, as most who have grown them will relate. So much so, that it is one of the dahlia's groups that is favoured by floral artists, and you can see collerette blooms gracing many of those exquisite exhibits at our summer flower shows.

Peony-flowered Dahlias

The peony dahlia, as already related in a previous chapter, was one of the forerunners of our modern decorative varieties. It is still very popular on the Continent, but not so much nowadays in Britain. Most of the few varieties available have broad, flat petals that rise loosely from the centre, which is often open or partly covered – resembling, in fact, the flower after which it is named. It grows somewhat lower than the other types, although not low enough, in truth, to qualify as a bedding dahlia. In practice, however, there are many growers who use this rare type as a bedding variety, and notwithstanding the fact that colours are limited, they find it a great addition to their summer plantings.

Decorative Dahlias

The decorative dahlia is one of the three main formations that are grown by gardeners today – the other two being the cactus forms and those that are grouped as Ball varieties. In formation, all should be possessed of a fully double centre showing no central disc at all. Usually the petals are flat or slightly involute (incurving), and sometimes there is a slight 'twist' in the petal length, adding an attraction to the group and a variation that can be most pleasing. In many examples, the involute petals also recurve as they mature, giving a globular effect and a fullness of bloom that pleases the showman – hence his or her attraction to this section. Conversely, petals can be straight, and this gives rise to a group within a group – those which are called 'water lily' dahlias, or to give them their official title – nymphaeas.

There are so many beautiful dahlias within the decorative groupings that it would be difficult to describe the impact that they have on the gardener who first encounters them. Whether the need is for stately and statuesque beauty for an elegant border, for long-stemmed blooms in a wide range of colour that can be cut for the home or, as so many enthusiasts choose, as a subject for exhibition, the decorative dahlia is a servant of all these needs. The decorative dahlias fall into the popular term of 'named' varieties, which simply means that each one grown commercially has been raised originally from seed and then

24

perpetuated vegetatively. You cannot grow a true decorative dahlia from seed saved from one season to the next. It is the hybrid influence again, and if you wish to have that beautiful scarlet or pastel pink dahlia you admired so much at a show or nursery, then it must be raised by a cutting or by a division of the tuber — which will be covered in a later chapter. Perhaps the most vital statistic that is recorded for the decorative dahlia is that it will grow to a width of 3 in. in many of the so-called miniature types whilst at the other end of the scale, massive blooms some 12 in. across can be grown — even by the beginner.

As the name suggests, this group produces blooms that are globular, with petals that reflex to the stem. All are fully double, and the florets are cupped in form, lying symmetrically around the firm centre to give a most pleasing effect when fully mature. It is this group that so fascinated our Victorian ancestors, who grew the type almost to the exclusion of other forms. They knew the Ball dahlia as the Double Show and Fancy — a name which, when broken down, means a full centre (double), a bloom of one colour only (show) or one that has a blend of several colours (fancy). It was this latter facet — the colour variation — that truly earned the devotion that nineteenth century gardeners gave, because the permutation of available hues — where reds and golds mixed with pinks and yellows — were so beguiling that every season brought a new crop of seedlings to maintain the fascination. Today the Ball dahlia still retains a fair share of the popularity that it enjoyed a century ago, but it is challenged most fervently in the hearts of true enthusiasts by the other forms available. Sizes in the Ball groups are limited, with groupings known simply as miniature Ball dahlias and Ball dahlias. The miniatures grow on plants around 3-4 ft in height, with blooms that do not usually exceed 4 in. in diameter. The Ball group come a little larger, flowering around 4-6 in. as a maximum. Perhaps the reason why this group stops at the 6 in.-mark is because the perfect geometrical formation of the petals, which gives the globular look, start to open out and are coarser when seen in varieties exceeding the

Ball Dahlias

6 in. top limit. Used for garden decoration, cut-flowers or exhibition, the colour range runs through the spectrum, with even a variety – *Bonnie Blue* – which attempts to claim that rare colour! Without success, it has to be said, because whilst the variety may carry the magic word 'blue' in its name, the National Dahlia Society's classification experts have catalogued this pretender as lilac!

Pompon
Dahlias

The pompon dahlia is, in effect, a miniaturisation of the Ball dahlia. It was discovered in the mid-1800s by the Germans, who gave it the name Lilliput. Not a bad choice in truth, but when French hybridists started to exploit the German raisings, they decided that it resembled the 'pompon' that adorns the hats of French sailors – and so it got its descriptive name. The true pompon should never grow more than 2 in. in diameter, and it is this fact that divides it from its bigger brothers, the Ball dahlias. Many gardeners will tell you that they are growing pompon dahlias, when they are in fact cultivating the Ball types. To make this dividing line more specific, the National Dahlia Society, having set the pompon size limit at 2 in. (or 52 mm) now issue a pom-ring of that measurement to its exhibitors and members, and any exhibit that even brushes this gauge is automatically disqualified. Perhaps our official body has good cause to keep the types permanently separate, because the form of the tiny pompon – often called the 'drumstick' dahlia – is sharper and more definite than the Ball dahlia. This is because of the size factor, of course, but the smaller petal formation does allow the pom a distinction that is denied in larger petalling types.

This lovely flower is most popular, and there are many who grow it to the exclusion of the other groups. That is not something that I should recommend, because one would be denied the pleasure of the other formations. For cut-flower work it is indispensable; it vases well and because of its tight form it lasts longer indoors. It is the choice of a whole army of enthusiasts who grow it world wide for exhibition, and there are men who have devoted their lives to its culture, not the least of whom was the Australian hybridiser, Norm Williams, who died in 1980 aged over 90. Mr Williams gave the world hundreds of pompons of great merit, and his famous prefix, Willo, lives on today, and will no doubt do so for years to come, in the dahlia catalogues of the world.

The pure cactus form, as opposed to the semi-cactus, is the variety known in gardeners' parlance as the 'spiky' dahlia. For the most part the petals are long, narrow and rolled, and can be straight or slightly incurving along their length. There are varieties in this group that will grow to a foot in diameter, whilst the miniature cactus attains widths of 4 in. or less. Average height of plants of this group is 3-4 ft and the colour range, like the other formations, contains every shade and variation of shades except pure blue.

It is amongst the smaller ranges of the cactus dahlias that many of our loveliest flowers appear. There is something about a vase of spiky cactus blooms that is particularly appealing. Perhaps it is the ease with which they can be arranged in the home that makes well-known types like the deep red *Doris Day* and the sulphur-yellow *Klankstad Kerkrade* so popular – a popularity that has been maintained for 20 years or more.

They are very easy to grow, and since this is the case, one would expect them to be more in evidence at our major flower shows. Unfortunately, this is not so, as in recent years they have succumbed to the pressures of the fuller-petalled semi-cactus types. Exhibition rules require a dahlia to be solidly built in form, and the finely quilled petals of the cactus dahlia, whilst being elegant and aristocratic, could never be accused of that.

There are exceptions, of course, and this occurs usually with the straight-petalled varieties. The British classification allows only for a wide-ranging group known simply as cactus, whereas in America, for example, the group is sub-divided into 'straight' and 'incurving' – thus allowing showmen to separate them on the showbench. The form originated in Holland with the chance discovery of a seedling with this narrow petal form. The original was given the name *D. Juarezii*, and all our modern varieties spring from this single source.

Semi-cactus Dahlias

The semi-cactus dahlia, as the name suggests, is half cactus and half something else. The something else is the decorative form which incorporates itself into this type to a point where, in many varieties, it predominates. There is no doubt that the combination of the two formations gives a bloom that is beautifully constructed. The inner petalling is broad-based (as on the decorative form) and narrows as the form continues along each floret, most ending in a decisive point. Full centres can be high and conical, giving a strength to the bloom in terms of depth and petal count that obviously attracts them to the exhibitor who has made this type a favourite for showbench work. With powerful stems and a fierce growth habit, the modern semi-cactus is capable of any role that it is asked to play. Again, the size range from the miniatures to the giants allows it to be used for garden decoration, cut-flowers or exhibition, and some of the largest dahlias in commercial growing today come into this adaptable section. In America varieties have been recorded as growing to a fantastic 18 in. in diameter, something that would rarely be seen in Europe, as the rules for exhibition in Britain, for example, insist that size must be allied with reasonable form (a balance of petals without inducing coarseness), and to achieve this means holding the bloom width to something around the 12 in. mark. It is a group to be recommended to the beginner — because first-class results can be achieved, even up to exhibition standard, with very few problems. The semi-cactus forms also offer a full range of colour, and some of the classical combinations like the scarlet-tipped white *Piquant* occur in this section. The form is also beloved of the Continental gardeners and in consequence many new introductions are raised by the Dutch, Belgian and French professionals in particular, and are grown widely in those countries, mainly for cut-flowers, as amateur exhibitions as we know them here do not exist on the Continent.

Miscellaneous Dahlias

How to describe a group of dahlias that contains everything, from tiny, star-like blooms just an inch across, to varieties that resemble the orchid and even the dahlia's arch rival, the chrysanthemum? To make a start I can introduce the tiniest of the dahlia forms, the so-called Lilliputs. A name taken from the past (remember it was the first name that the modern pompon was given), these low-growing, inch-wide dahlias are open-centred and bloom in profusion. They are ideal for using on patios in pot or tub culture, and can be grown as bedding types, edging a lawn or flower bed effectively and with a wide colour variation. The orchid dahlias, like their contemporaries the chrysanthemum-flowered varieties, obtained their descriptive titles from the fact that their forms resemble very closely the flowers they tend to imitate. Both are rare, with just a handful of varieties available through the trade. It would be fair to say that the orchid varieties are the better-known types, such as the elegant *Giraffe* (a combination of yellow and russet brown) and are widely grown for floral artwork. There are also dahlias that resemble the carnation, with split petal ends (known as fimbriation) that look for all the world like our popular wedding flower, the carnation, and others that look similar to the rose. Looking very like an opening rosebud, in the mature formation, the latter originated in Japan and have never really caught on with the British public. The anemone, peony and water-lily forms have been described already, as they have all been given groups to themselves, but the combination of the imitative forms gives ample weight to the fact that the miscellaneous group of dahlias has been called the chameleon of the horticultural world. Every so often a new form arrives, most recently it has been a miniature collerette (again from Japan) and a needle-pointed variety that looks for all the world like a rayonante chrysanthemum. There is no doubt that the repertoire of this flower is far from exhausted, and the future holds a great deal for the hybridist explorers who delight in stretching this species to its limits and even beyond. Mutations have even been achieved by exposing tubers to gamma rays, and the results were rewarding, although not in a commercial sense.

What does the future hold? Well there is that blue dahlia I have mentioned; and we are still seeking a dahlia with a decent scent (that surely is the next step); and the variety that is partially frost resistant, to give the dahlia an extended season, is awaited eagerly. Who can say, all these things and more could well be achieved in the next 20 years by enthusiasts as yet unknown.

CHAPTER 3

Propagation

There are three methods of propagating the dahlia —
by the sowing of seed, the division of the roots or tubers
and the taking of cuttings from overwintered stock.
Each method has its advantages and disadvantages, and
all three give similar results. The fact that the gardener
may choose from the three or even adapt them all to
his or her needs is a valuable asset, because they relate
to the time available, the sort of equipment that is
needed and, of course, to the space that is available
for the plants — the eventual end product of all the
methods.

It would be extremely difficult to say which of the
propagating methods was the most popular. Seed sowing,
because of its economy might well stand as the leading
candidate, but that would be to assume the results that
can be obtained by this method and deny the fact that
the nursery trade, producing dahlia stock every spring
from cuttings, creates millions of new plants for sale.
Many more millions are held in the form of stock roots
that can be purchased by the gardener in the autumn,
a miniaturised tuber (known as a pot tuber or root),
that the trade offers in the dark days of winter when
sales of other forms are not available. This method is
successful and has been for many years, with total sales
figures for countries like Holland and Belgium, for
example, exceeding 50 million every autumn. Among
amateur gardeners, however, the division of an old dahlia
tuber would still seem to be an evergreen favourite. It

requires little equipment, rather less time and, most importantly, a lot less in terms of cash outlay.

Comparing performances of the three methods is somewhat relative, as each will offer sturdy plants for summer planting that will give excellent results. And after all, need and ambition play a great part in this, because what rates as a good dahlia display in the eyes of one gardener might well be considered second class by another. The reason for this is, naturally, the variance of form, colour, plant height and productivity, which gives a choice so wide that two growers may never plant the same types of dahlia in a whole lifetime of gardening. Certainly in 30 years of dahlia gardening, I have yet to find two plots that are identical. A rose garden or a planting of gladiolus; a summer bedding scheme or a bed of carnations, may all look exactly alike in a thousand suburban gardens, but the dahlia plot never will.

To examine the three methods of propagation in more detail needs the basic understanding of the stock that makes this possible. All dahlia plants come from one of two sources, viz. seed saved from the previous season or tubers that have been overwintered. Seed is harvested in the autumn and stored until it is sown in the spring. Tubers, because of their inability to survive a hard winter, are lifted soon after the first frosts, cleaned and stored in readiness for their re-employment in the next season. With one or both of these propagation basics available, the gardener is in a position to produce a whole crop of dahlia plants in the few short weeks of spring — many more than he or she will need for personal use, which is one of the unfading reasons for the popularity of the dahlia, notwithstanding its dislike of our hard winters. Below is a detailed analysis of the three methods of propagation.

Seed Sowing

The dahlia produces seed quite easily, and the conical seed heads that follow the fading of the bloom will ripen readily in September and October. When it is obvious that they have matured, they must be taken from the plant and allowed a week or two indoors to dry out completely. In order to do this effectively and produce a batch of these tiny, black, easy to handle seeds, it is advisable to cut open the pods and lay them in shallow trays in a sunny position. The husks will then turn crisp and dry, leaving the seed perkily disposed amongst this chaff, and ready to be extracted.

Seed extraction is one of the truly fiddly jobs of the whole dahlia year, but a patient hour with your seed heads will result in a neat separation, so that when you have enough seed for your needs they can be stored in sealed containers. Strong envelopes, preferably marked with the name or type of the parent, are suitable, or you can seal them into airtight tins, where they will remain until you need them. If you do not have dahlia plants from which this initial seed is obtainable, then you will find that they are readily available through the trade. Most general nurseries sell dahlia seed, and nowadays it can be bought in type. For example, bedding dahlia seed, in a variety of proprietary names like Coltness Gem or the recent Redskin mixtures will offer seed to produce plants for your summer bedding schemes. Cactus, Decorative and Ball/Pompon seed, so marked and marketed by main seed suppliers or specialist dahlia centres, will give results that might produce a wealth of blooms of the types marked on the packet. In truth, however, the results of plants raised from such seed is somewhat limited in success value by the simple fact that the dahlia is and always has been a natural hybrid. This means that so-called decorative seeds will produce cactus or semi-cactus forms, and, of course, vice versa. There are many who do not mind this state of affairs, because among this air of uncertainty as to the final result, lies the possibility that a truly magnificent new variety can be raised in the amateur's garden. Just anyone has the chance of finding this pearl in the oyster — and it is by this method that almost all new dahlias arrive, in fact the amateur raiser reigns supreme in the world of new dahlias, and with the exception of a few professional traders, particularly on the Continent, all our new varieties started as a gleam in some amateur dahlia grower's eye!

If your need then is for dahlias to fill a border or a mixed collection of unknown value, the seed sowing is for

Figure 3.1
Spraying Plants in
the Cold Frame

you. To make a start requires very little equipment. Dahlia
seedlings can be raised in a greenhouse – heated or
unheated. Success can be achieved in a coldframe on a
sunny windowsill or even on a patio if covered initially
with polythene or glass. This wide choice of facilities
means also that you can start any time from February
onwards, with the aim of producing a batch of young,
sturdy seedlings by the end of May or early June to coin-
cide with the accepted time for planting in the open
garden – late May, when all fear of a frost should have
passed. The earlier you start, of course, the longer you
have to look after the young newcomers, as growth after
germination is very rapid. By starting, say, in February,
you will need to use a heated greenhouse, but by sowing
in March or early April, no heat is required. Mid April,
and you can sow in a coldframe, and from late April until
mid-May dahlia seed will successfully germinate in a sunny

window or on the patio covered with a sheet of glass or polythene. The later that you start, of course, means that logically you will have later blooms. However, this is not always the case, as summer weather varies so dramatically at times that even late plants can catch up with those raised much earlier in the year.

If we look at a midway exercise in seed sowing, this means that you could sow dahlia seed in an unheated greenhouse in April. For this, use the normal shallow seed trays, and a good, sterilised seed compost. The value of this is that the young dahlia seedlings will not be confused with weed seedlings when they eventually emerge — and, of course, there is little risk of infection in a sterilised medium. Sow the seeds about an inch apart, which means that you will get 40-50 in a standard seed tray. Prepare the seed-sowing compost carefully, making sure that it is moist as opposed to being sodden with moisture. If you do this, then no further watering is necessary. Press the seed into the surface of the medium, and then cover with a further 0.25 in. of the same compost. A piece of glass over the tray, shaded with a sheet of brown paper, will hasten the arrival of the seedlings, and it is essential to turn and wipe the glass at least once a day to avoid damping off — a fungus attack that will rot the tiny seedlings if not countered.

Germination takes about a week — longer if the weather is inclement. As the new arrivals develop and put on their first true pair of leaves, you can move them on into something a little more substantial than the seed-sowing compost in which they have started life. Use a good soilless compost for this, or a potting compost based on the John Innes formula — No. 1 (the lowest fertiliser rating) is sufficient for these youngsters. The move can be into deeper trays (tomato trays are perfect) or into individual pots — say 3 in. size. Transfer each one carefully, and gently firm the roots. A tomato tray will hold about 20 young seedlings if they are spaced 3-4 in. apart. If you use pots, then, of course, just transfer one seedling to each.

For the first few days after this initial move, keep the pots and trays well shaded. Bright sunlight will wilt the seedlings and if this happens it is very difficult to get them to stand upright again. After this initial care, the young plants, because that is what they have now become, will virtually take care of themselves — so self-sufficient is this flower.

If you have raised seedlings in a cold greenhouse or a coldframe, then they should not require hardening off before planting in the open garden. But care must be taken to protect them from frost at all times — and it is not until the magic time of late May or early June, when those frosts have disappeared for the summer, than you can plant out in the open. With a crop of young dahlia seedlings in trays or pots, you are in a position to fill your garden with colour with very little attention — they will need some summer care of course, but more about that in a later chapter.

Raising Dahlia Plants from Cuttings

Creating dahlia plants from cuttings taken from the old tubers — or to give it its correct name, vegetative propagation — has one distinct advantage over seed sowing, it reproduces exactly the variety from which the cutting is taken. This means, of course, that the elegant scarlet cactus or pink pompon that you admire so much one year, can be grown again in perfect replica the next. Thus dahlias assume a continuity, and varieties perpetuated in this way are called 'named' dahlias. Some 20,000 are officially listed, with many tens of thousands more grown world wide.

Naturally, the cutting method allows you to select the sort of colours that you might wish your dahlia plot to produce; the sort of form that you prefer, the height and productivity; in fact all the things that make gardening more selective and, indeed, more pleasurable. To make a start on this method means, in truth, the possession of some basic equipment. If your aim is to produce a fair quantity of cuttings, then you will need to make a start in late February or early March, and this means the use of a heated greenhouse. If you have some overwintered dahlia tubers in store, then you will be ready to begin. On the other hand, if you have to acquire stock, then a whole army of suppliers will be ready to offer you the wherewithal to fill your garden.

Most nurserymen list dahlia tubers that can be bought from November until around the end of March. Specialist dahlia establishments produce lavish catalogues to tempt you, and the overseas sources are legion, with dahlia tubers these days coming from the Common Market (notably the Dutch, French, Belgians and Germans) but with a wide choice also offered from the United States, Canada, Australia and New Zealand, to name but a few of the mainstream suppliers.

Tubers, or roots as they are sometimes called, are sold in one of two forms, the so-called field tuber and the pot tuber. The field tuber or root is one that has been grown in the open throughout the previous season and is usually much larger than the pot tuber. The pot tuber or pot root, as mentioned briefly earlier, obtains its name from the simple fact that it has been grown the previous season within the confines of a small pot. This has the effect of restricting dramatically the size of the root, with obvious connotations. The reduction in bulk makes for easier handling and storage; packaging and despatch charges are reduced because of the weight difference and, most important of all, they are small enough to be sent rapidly by airmail from one end of the world to the other. Thus the tuber these days becomes the main exchange unit for both the trade (who exchange for cash) and the amateur who swops his stock with friends in every corner of the dahlia growing world.

With a supply of your favourite dahlia tubers available, it is advisable to warm up your greenhouse for a few days before taking your tubers out of store or from the boxes in which they have been delivered. You will need some reasonable compost in which to grow the roots that will produce the cuttings, and so warm up this at the same time. Depending on the size of your stock roots, prepare trays or boxes about 4 in. in depth, filling them with a good loam — leaf-mould, peat and soil mixes or soilless compost are a few suggestions, with the accent being on a medium that is open and drains freely. Water the prepared containers well, and allow them to drain on the staging for a day or two before committing the tubers.

The tubers may now be 'set up' in the trays, an expression used by dahlia growers which has a particular meaning. Setting up your roots means partially submerging them into the surface of the compost you have prepared to a point where the crown of each root joins the fat, tuberous portions. The reason for this is to prevent rot setting in, something that will very quickly spread and damage or, in extreme cases, destroy the tubers before they get a chance to grow. Additionally, the greater majority of the new shoots that will eventually become the cuttings you are aiming to produce, emanate from the crown of each root, and by having these clear of the wet surface of your compost, danger of disease is minimised. With your tubers set up in the compost, it requires only that you maintain a good temperature in your greenhouse. In early March, nights can be bitterly cold, so the thermometer should never be allowed to drop below 50°F (10°C). If you are able to maintain these night temperatures, then the first 'eyes' or shoots will show themselves on the crown within 14 days — sometimes a little longer, dependent upon the varieties that you choose to grow. If you are using pot tubers as opposed to the large field roots, then you will find that these tiny dahlia tubers are much quicker in sending out growth points than are their bigger brethren. The reason for this is that the root on the pot tuber develops more rapidly (through the restricting growth of the previous summer) and the shoots respond accordingly.

When the new growth has shown itself, it is a matter of days before it elongates into a length that is substantial enough to offer cuttings. The ideal length is 3-4 in., and when this has been achieved, the cutting is ready to be removed from the parent plant and roots induced to grow on an erstwhile naked stem, thus turning the cutting into a fully fledged dahlia plant.

For successful rooting, you will need a continuance of the heat that has given you the cuttings and a propagating area within the greenhouse that gives initial protection to the cuttings. A compost is also needed that is somewhat different from what the tubers were set up in. Cuttings will develop roots in trays or boxes of a rooting medium on the

Figure 3.2 Taking
Cuttings for
Rooting

open greenhouse staging, but better results will be obtained
if a small propagator is used. You can buy these, of course,
which warm the soil by electric cables, or you can make
one quite easily for yourself. The idea is to create a moist
atmosphere, with a higher temperature than the rest of the
greenhouse, in which the cuttings will be encouraged to
grow roots. A small box, taller at the rear than the front
(to allow excess moisture to run away) about 3 ft x 2 ft is
enough for most amateurs' needs, and this should have a
lid, preferably hinged, that is made of glass or polythene.
Set the propagating box or frame over your heat source,
and cover the base with a few inches of moist peat. On to
this, place trays or small pots filled with a rooting mixture,
and here you have a wide choice. Dahlias will root in
almost any medium, just so long as it is free draining. By
far the most popular is a 50/50 mixture of fine peat and
silver sand (or small grade potting sand). Other mediums
that produce healthy roots are soilless cuttings compost,
vermiculite, pure sand or permutations of each one. If you
are unsure of the best rooting compost for your particular
needs, then experiment with them until you find the one
that suits you best.

Whichever medium you choose, make sure that it is moist before it is put into the pots or trays. Firm it well, and level the surface fractionally below the level of the container. Now place the pots and trays into the propagator, submerging them just an inch or so into the peat base. In this way, they will benefit from the rising heat (or 'bottom' heat as it is sometimes called) — a situation that is conducive to trouble-free rooting. With the propagating box and rooting compost prepared, you are now in a position to turn your attention to the cuttings.

By now your tubers should be offering a ready supply of cuttings, and remembering the ideal length of 3-4 in., they can be separated from the parent root. This can be done in one of two ways: by gently bending the shoot, you will find that it comes away easily, taking with it a small portion of the growth eye base. These are known as untrimmed cuttings, and root easier than cuttings severed with a sharp knife. The disadvantage of this method, however, is that by taking the whole growth point you often deny the root the chance to offer further cuttings from that source. However, should your needs be minimal, then this is certainly a good way to take the cuttings. With quantity in mind, the cuttings should be treated differently, and this means severing them cleanly from the old tuber, with a knife or razor blade, at a point just fractionally above the eye. This method ensures that you will have more cuttings from that particular point, and if you want a lot of plants or, maybe, your initial rooting is not successful, then you have an insurance against this.

With your supply of cuttings to hand, and the propagator in position, the miracle of rooting is about to happen. I never fail to marvel at this act of reproduction which, in practice, is so simple. All that is necessary is for the cuttings to be trimmed immediately below a leaf node and then dipped into a rooting powder. They are then inserted into the prepared pots or trays, about an inch deep, and placed inside the propagating box. Nature, then, does the rest.

The development of root on each separate shoot takes about 14 days in February or March — rather less in April and May. It is patently obvious when fresh root has

Figure 3.3
Cuttings in a
Propagator

Figure 3.4
Cuttings Take
about 14 Days
to Root

Figure 3.5 Good
and Bad Cuttings

emerged from the bare stem, as the cuttings perk up
happily and just shout that they are now plants. Occa-
sionally, there are some outside interferences that delay or
mar your success. Damping off — a fungus that rots the
young shoots — will occur if conditions are too moist, and
this can be remedied by opening the frame an inch or two
to allow more air. Wilting, that is a collapse of the shoots
in the pots or trays, will happen if you allow too much
bright sunlight into the propagator, and this can be countered by shading the lid on occasions when the days are
sunny. An overhead spray with water given early in the
morning or late at night will also help to revive those
cuttings that persist in lying down.

But back to those perky youngsters that are sending out
new roots. They will not wish to remain in the rooting
medium very long, for the one reason that there is little
nutrient for them to absorb and so grow on strongly. You

Figure 3.6
Cuttings
Straight from
the Propagator

Figure 3.7
Freshly-potted
Cuttings

Figure 3.8
Completed Pot
of Cuttings

must provide this, and it means moving the new plants into pots or boxes that can offer something substantial in the way of feed. Nowadays, many gardeners prefer to use the efficient soilless compost, which is basically peat and fertiliser. It is easy to handle and guarantees your plants' well being. Alternatively, the proven John Innes composts can be bought for potting on the young dahlias, and here it is advisable to choose either JI No. 1, if you are potting on in April or May, or No. 2 if you pot earlier than these months; a provision that will give your plants a greater availability of nutrient over the longer period that you are caring for them.

Ideally, strong-growing young dahlias prefer to be potted — and if 3 or 3.5 inch plastic or crock pots are used, then they will survive without any possibility of hindrance for several weeks until needed for planting in the open garden. Deep trays, of course, are acceptable, but the disadvantage here is that the extra room allows the roots of several plants to intermingle, and if you have ever tried to extricate trays full of roots at planting time without damaging at least some of them, then you will understand just why individual pots are my recommendation.

Once the new plants have been transferred into a good potting compost, they should be placed on the greenhouse staging away from the main heat source. This lowering of the temperature in which they are being asked to grow, steadies them down and helps to make a short-stemmed, wide-leafed plant that in the long term is the best possible plant form for producing maximum bloom. Later, say in late April or May, the pots or trays can be moved into the coldframe. Here they will encounter a further lowering of temperature, and it is this gradual reduction that produces a hardy plant — they may even resist a degree or two of frost if asked to do so. The whole process is known as 'hardening off', and not only is it a method of producing well-formed, hardy young dahlia plants, but because they are prepared for almost anything, and receive no check at all when set out in the open garden, the bonus that you receive for the care you have taken is a crop of dahlia blooms much earlier than normal. And that, in terms of flower quantity, can mean several hundred extra dahlias over the full season.

The third, and I suspect the truly popular method of dahlia propagation, is the production of plants from a simple division of the old roots. For most, it is enough to create, say, three or four plants where only one grew before, and this is easily achieved by most overwintered dahlia tubers. A dahlia root has the happy knack of producing growth points or eyes, usually in abundance and normally well-spaced around the crown, the part of the tuber which is located as a bulge or prominence where the old stem and the fattened part of the root meet. It is these shoots that will make the separate plants, and the splitting or division of the whole tuber into several portions has only small requirements for success, and that is for the splits to be possessed of a good strong shoot (or more than one)

Raising Dahlia Plants from Tuber Divisions

45

Figure 3.9
A Well-grown
Dahlia Tuber

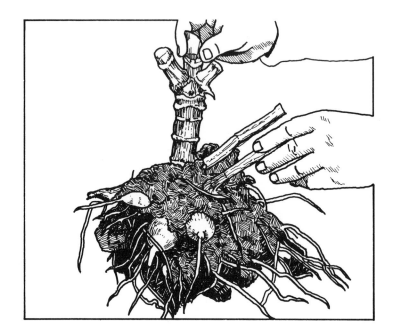

Figure 3.10
Dahlia Tubers:
Before Being
Plunged for
Cuttings

and a piece of the old root.

The most expeditious way to obtain the best from a divided tuber is to firstly allow the growth points to identify themselves. This is sometimes achieved naturally during storage, and when the dahlia root is taken from store in April or May, they appear as small, white dots on the crown. Naturally, the eyes lack normal colour because they have been stored in the dark, but a few days on the staging of your greenhouse or in a coldframe, and they will assume the deep, green hues that we associate with good development, and will be ready for splitting.

If the tuber has no signs of growth or perhaps is a late-starting variety, then you can produce the eyes very quickly by plunging the tubers, crown deep, in a good, open compost — say leaf-mould, peat or soilless compost. Water the plunged roots well, and keep them free from frost if in a greenhouse or frame. Within two weeks your dahlias will be bursting with life and promise and the division can begin. Make the initial split by cutting cleanly through the centre of the old stem and on through the fleshy parts of the root, aiming as you do between the two best shoots. With the tuber in two parts, further sub-divisions can be made, again via the old stem, just so long as each piece that you take has those all important ingre-dients — a growth eye and a bit of the old root.

Each division that you make will become a fully blown plant in due course and, in the space of a single summer, offer a full crop of blooms with another large tuber in the autumn for you to continue as before. To effect this, however, you must offer the divisions a good start in life, and that means providing each one with the wherewithal to grow healthily. If the divisions are large, use deep boxes or large pots to hold them, and provide either soilless compost or J.I. potting compost No. 1 in which the new roots can delve. If the splits are made in late April (the best time) or May, then they will have plenty of time to elongate and flourish before they can be planted out in the open garden in early June. During all this period, they must be protected from frost, but allowed maximum sunshine and regular watering, open up the greenhouse or frame on sunny spring days, and close it at night if the

Figure 3.11
Selecting Plants

temperature drops towards freezing. As an added bonus to the division method of propagation, it is often possible to further divide the splits you have already made after a week or two in their new quarters. The extra root that develops and the new shoots that appear, will give the watchful gardener a chance to obtain further plants by taking away yet more growth — all of which will grow and produce a full crop of dahlias, as long as the golden rule of new shoot and root portion is remembered. One important point that must be made is that unlike potatoes, absolutely no growth will come from the fat, tuberous pieces of the dahlia tuber. New plants can only come from the growth that starts on the crown.

Summing Up   With the three methods of dahlia propagation described, you simply take your choice. Each will give you a colourful summer with bloom in profusion, and depending on your personal ambitions, provide you with cut flowers, blooms for your pleasure and garden enhancement or, should you wish, quality flowers that will win you prizes at your local flower show. In any or all of these things, you have one ally, the dahlia. It just wants to propagate itself, and even if you stray from the guided paths I have indicated, then it will compensate, which means that even the complete novice can enter into the realms of propagation without any fears at all.

CHAPTER 4

Cultivation

It has to be said at the outset, that the dahlia's needs in terms of attention and fertilisation are few, for it will grow in almost any soil and situation and virtually in any extremes of weather with, of course, the notable exception

Figure 4.1
Selecting Plants

of frosts, which it vehemently hates. But having said all that, and by the same yardstick that the good gardener uses to produce the very best from whatever subject he or she is growing, a little consideration or even on occasions, cosseting, will bring rich rewards in longer flowering, better productivity and in the case of the really keen grower, improved quality.

If we accept, as we must, that the dahlia will grow virtually in any soil and situation, then there are obviously soils and positions in your garden that the dahlia would not prefer. For example, a badly drained plot, where rain will lie for long periods, is just about the worst place that you could choose, as the rampant root system that this genus develops needs a well-drained position, and if you offer something less than that, the dahlia will show its resentment by poor performance. Again, the vital growth factor that the dahlia displays, whereby a young seedling just a few inches high can within the space of a few short summer weeks become a massive bush some 6 ft high and 12 ft in circumference, means that an open, sunlit plot is the best to choose. If you position your dahlia plants alongside a high wall, near to high shrubs or under the spread of tall trees, the growth will be drawn and skinny, offering flowers of the same ilk. Avoid such places, and select a spot in your garden that is well drained, open and receives a fair proportion of the day's offering of summer sunshine.

For most gardeners, the sort of soil that they have in their garden is rarely chosen personally. If you have heavy clay, then you will be well aware of the problems as, indeed, will those who garden on light soils that seem to dry out after one day's sunshine. Ideally, the dahlia likes a reasonably heavy soil, and if you have a clay medium, then you can bring this into line with the ideal by incorporating good compost, manures or other bulk additives to open it up. Similarly, stable or farmyard manure, peat, spent hops or compost added to a light soil will give the necessary moisture retention without holding water to the detriment of the dahlia's well-being. If you add to these basic requirements, a full season's support in the form of well-planned maintenance, then you are three parts of the

Cultivation

way to becoming the owner of the perfect dahlia garden.
Let's look at these seasonal cultural needs in more detail.

Autumn and
Spring Soil
Preparation

In truth, a dahlia season starts just as soon as the plants
from the previous summer have been frosted, and the
tubers lifted for winter storage, a subject which will be
dealt with in a later chapter. With the plot or border clear,
the chance must be taken to turn over the soil for the
winter. There is no need at all for double digging – often
advocated for this flower – a single spit's depth, turned
and angled for maximum exposure is all that you need to
do. The roots of a dahlia plant spread widely and massively
in that top spade's depth, and it is this that should receive
the full benefit of your autumn labours. If the single spit
is slightly raised as you dig, then the surface will receive
nature's own renewal process, a cleansing by winter frost,
and that is something that offers real value to the plot in
terms of a friable and smooth crumbling of the soil structure, in which the planting of the young dahlias in late
May becomes an absolute pleasure.

At the time that you start on the autumn dig, endeavour
to add to the plot some of the goodness that the season
has removed. It would be easy to say dig in as much stable
farmyard manure as you can, but like so many modern
gardeners, I have found that the acquisition of this five-star
commodity becomes more and more difficult, so my
remedy is to make something for myself that is equally as
good. By this I mean well-rotted compost made in your
own garden, and I have been producing cubic yards of this
for the last 30 years, and my plot revels in it. Nothing is
wasted in the garden or home, and my wife must have
walked hundreds of miles to and from the compost heap
over the years as she adds the waste that every kitchen
turns out daily. Add to this produce of the garden in
terms of grass clippings, turf edgings, old plants, autumn
leaves, in fact almost everything with the exception of
woody clippings, evergreen or diseased plants and the heap
multiplies at a fascinating rate. I reckon to achieve a large
compost heap, with enough material to cover my dahlia
plot completely to a depth of 2-3 in., at least twice a year.

52

This means that you must pay as much heed to the requirements of your compost heap as you do the other subjects
in your garden. Too often, the compost heap is treated
with indifference, when in fact it is an important asset to
your garden. For twice-yearly bonuses from my spot
under the apple tree, I need to exercise good husbandry,
which means turning regularly, and using one of the
modern compost activators. I choose one that adds nitrogen to the heap, and it is layered alternatively with 6 in. of
soil, a foot of garden and kitchen refuse, onto which is
sprinkled liberal helpings of the activator. Result: rich,
crumbly goodness for the price of a few hours' labour.

All of this free fertiliser is incorporated into the dahlia
plot in the autumn, and in addition to raising the nutrient
quotient in the soil, it encourages earthworms to flourish
which, in their turn, make the whole plot rich and free-
draining. One further valuable contribution that the
autumn dig and compost addition make in a natural way,
is raising the level of the soil. If your garden is low lying
and holds moisture overlong, then there is no better way
of remedying the situation than by building up the plot.
If you think that your dahlia garden will eventually be
several feet above normal with these yearly contributions,
then let me disillusion you. My garden now stands some
10 in. above the lowest level, which is partly retained by
boarding the outer edges. All of this has taken about 30
years, and in return for all that goodness returned to the
soil, my reward has been the thousands of blooms that it
has been my pleasure to grow. With the plot neatly dug
for the winter, it should need no further attention until
the spring, and the time to start is in late March or early
April, when the first warmth of the early spring sunshine
entices both you and the soil to work well together. It is
of little value getting on to the plot too early when the
ground is still heavy with winter rains. Better to wait until
the plot turns easily with a spade or fork; any other time
and you might well damage the structure you have carefully nurtured through the autumn and winter.

The spring dig is the easiest of tasks if you have laid the
foundations the previous autumn. A light forking, or
spading on heavier soils, will bring the soil down beautifully,

Figure 4.2
Preparing the
Dahlia Plot

Figure 4.3
Dahlia Tuber

and the time is right to add a little more organic goodness, this time in the form of bonemeal, a long acting fertiliser that the dahlia loves. Rather than scatter the bonemeal willy-nilly, work out your requirements per square yard, basing the need on a formula of 4 oz. to each. It is an easy thing to get this right, by marking off the area with canes in a squared pattern and then adding the recommended amount to the correct soil area. Choose a day when the air is still to scatter the bonemeal on to the surface of your dahlia plot, and gently fork it into the top few inches. Nature will then do the rest, taking it down to where it will become readily available to the dahlia roots. The dahlia plot is now ready to give you a superb performance, and as April stretches into May, it is time to think about preparing for planting out.

As described in the previous chapter, dahlia plants can be **Planting Out** one of three types — raised from seed, taken from cuttings or division of tubers. It does not matter into which category your own plants come, the all-important rule is that none of these should be set in the open garden before all fear of frost is over. There are no more anxious eyes in late May and early June than those of the keen dahlia grower, who watches the clearing skies in the evening with apprehension and listens to every weather forecast with rapt attention! There is good reason for all of this, as a few degrees of late spring frost will at best damage and check young plants and at worst cut them back so badly that they never perform effectively at all. The single exception to this golden rule of frost evasion is the planting of non-sprouted tubers. Many growers choose this method, and it entails the planting of roots or tubers that have not displayed growth eyes on the crown or perhaps have small embryo shoots just opening. Tubers of this sort can be planted in early May, and the crown set 4-5 in. below the level of the soil. By the time that the new growth does emerge to face the rigours of a British summer, frosts are usually over and development continues without interference. Re-planted tubers, however, have the disadvantage of needing to create a new root system and, by producing several growth shoots, often lack the quality that is achieved by the other methods of propagation. Conversely, a warm May will hasten the dormant tubers into rapid growth, and if this happens the dahlia shoots, like a planting of early potatoes, will break surface at a time when frosts are still likely. Here instant remedial action is necessary, and protruding growth should be protected at night from frost damage by covering with large pots, cardboard boxes or a fair depth of dry straw. And it is not unknown for frosts to linger irritatingly into the early weeks of June, and should this happen, even the optimistically planted divisions, seedlings or rooted cuttings should have the same night protection.

When it is considered safe to proceed, the next step is to allocate a spot on the dahlia plot for each plant. Ideally, the dahlia likes plenty of room, with at least 2 ft between the smaller-flowering types and more — say up to 3 ft, between each plant of the large and giant varieties. Only the bedding dahlias will enjoy less space, and if these are to be set around a border or *en masse* in a centrally situated flower bed, a distance of 9-12 in. between each should be allowed.

To make sure that you have enough room to accommodate all your plants, mark out the bed beforehand with canes. This marker-cane system can serve as your guide when planting out, and as the first of several supports that the taller growing dahlias will require later on. If possible set the canes at the recommended distances in double rows, with a wider distance between each set of canes to allow for free passage during the summer when the foliage is dominant and jobs like tying, watering, spraying and feeding are essential. At each cane base, a planting hole can be extracted, large enough to accommodate the root ball or division, plus roots, of your dahlia plants. Into each hole, place a good double handful of moist peat or, if you are feeling extravagant, soilless compost. This planting 'bed' ensures a lively start for the dahlias, and the first probing roots find something extra special in which to delve. The plants can now be set on the prepared plot, and it is advisable to position the level of your root ball an inch or so below the level of the garden soil. In this way, as the

Figure 4.4
Spacing Out
for Planting

Figure 4.5
Setting Out
Young Dahlia
Plants

plant is firmed home, a slight depression is created that will be useful for watering in the early stages of development. All that is required now is for overlong plants to be loosely tied in to the marker cane, thus preventing them 'swinging' and possibly being damaged.

For a few weeks after completing this planting, there is little to do on the plot except to keep it weed free and well hoed. A watch should also be kept for predators, and there are none worse than the insidious slug and snail on a warm June evening, which feel that the succulent young growth of your dahlia plants is there especially for them. Prevent the incursions of these molluscs by baiting the whole plot with slug pellets or bran. This deterrent is laced with metaldehyde, something that the slugs and snails find irresistible, and is lethal. Heavy infestations can be controlled by using the same chemical diluted in water, which is applied to the area in the vicinity of the plants and, effectively, not only destroys the larger beasties, but kills off the smaller, more difficult young slugs. I shall deal more fully with the control of pests and the prevention of diseases in another chapter, suffice now to say that this is one of the most dangerous periods for your plants during the year. As the year progresses towards the end of June, those who have been conscientiously wielding the hoe to keep the plot clean will find that small fragments of roots are being cut almost at ground level. This is nature's signal that the hoeing can stop, as the first mass movement of root is spreading outwards from the plant to eventually fill the whole of the surrounding area. Before this is accomplished, there are several jobs that need to be done. Firstly, the chance should be taken to insert the extra support for the strong-growing plants. Soon they will be stretching rapidly upwards as more nutrient is taken in by that rampant root system. To contain this growth, add two more 4 ft canes at the front of each plant, thus making a triangle within which the plants can grow and, at the same time, be firmly controlled by tying in the whole structure with twine or raffia. The 'cage' that is so formed will suffice for a whole season and apart from stringing back other branches that stray from the supports, the effect is to reduce maintenance to a minimum.

Next, as that surface-root system races out, is the provision of some form of encouragement. Surface-rooting plants need this, and if a ground covering or mulch is provided, then not only will the roots spread even further, but if the right sort of mulch material is used, then they will rise from the original soil level into the extra layer, thus obtaining additional nutrient. There is of course a wide choice of mulch: well-rotted compost, stable or farmyard manures (similarly weathered), peat or spent hops or even the summer lawn clippings, just so long as a depth of only an inch or so is used with the latter. Ideally, 3-4 in. of cover should be aimed at, and if you are unable to provide something that will offer root protection *and* nutrient, then cover the soil with straw, which is the best substitute. Take your chosen material close to the stems of the plants without actually touching them, and this will give you an added benefit — that of moisture conservation.

Before we leave June — there is one other need that your plantings may require — water. After the initial setting out in the open garden, it takes a week or two for the root ball to unwind and send out roots to look for water and food. In a dry June, make sure that this is on hand, either by watering directly from a can to the depression that you made when planting or by watering overhead with a hose or spray-lines at regular intervals. The dahlia is 95 per cent water, and if it fails to absorb enough, then the structure suffers, which in its turn affects the number of blooms that you will get later in the season.

Towards the end of June and into the first weeks of July, it is necessary to help the plant a little by encouraging the side-shoots that will bear the first bloom to hasten along. This is done by a simple expedient known as 'stopping'. A strange term, because it means exactly the opposite. Stopping, or the removal of the main growing tip of each plant, directs the energies into the side-shoots, and they respond accordingly. The operation is a simple one — take the central shoot, and bend it gently, when you will find that it snaps away readily. Within a week you will see the difference: those side shoots, nestling in each leaf axil, will fatten and elongate, each one destined to be a dahlia. Stopping can be carried out on all types of dahlia, including

Figure 4.6
Tying in the
Dahlias

the seed-sown bedding varieties. With these, the effect is to mass up the naturally low-growing plants into a continuous band of bloom and colour, and if they are set out as suggested, around 9-12 in. apart, then the blooms intermingle and in addition to the spectacular show that you are treated to, they need no support at all.

Taller-growing varieties however do need support, and if you have used the three-cane 'cage' system, then as the side shoots lengthen and the stems thicken, they must be contained, otherwise summer's natural hazards of wind and rain will bend or even snap them off. As this first flush of bloom develops, secure them inside the triangle of canes or, if they tend to stray outside as many will, tie them close in to one of the trio of supports.

By now, the season is getting very close to offering you the first dahlias, and the signs that you get are unmistakable. At the end of each rising stem a small, compact bud cluster will form. As this opens out, you will find a central or leading bud, which is rather fatter than the two others positioned slightly below. The main bud will always flower before these ancillary buds, and if left to their own devices, they will open in the form of a spray rather than a single, well-stemmed dahlia. Many growers prefer this form of cultivation, although it is fair to comment that it does have its disadvantages. For example the central bloom, denied the full benefit of the rising goodness, is lesser in size and almost certainly reduced in quality, at least where fullness of form is concerned. The smaller buds will also have very short stems, and if required for arrangements in the home would be difficult to display effectively. Naturally, if you are the sort of gardener who just hates cutting flowers from your garden, then the spray or bud cluster is excellent, and for overall colour, mass and effect cannot be bettered. If you wish to cut your dahlias for the home or for the pleasure your friends will have in receiving them, then the method is simple and does no harm to the plant as many believe, in fact the reverse is true — the plants actually derive benefit. To create the longer stem, remove those two smaller buds in the cluster, leaving just the main bud

Figure 4.7
Disbudding

to flower. This will give you a better quality dahlia and a stem some 14-18 in. long on most varieties.

To obtain longer stem length, remove also the two shoots that you will find nestling in the next leaf axil further down the main stem. You will find that you can readily cut flowers much bigger than you have ever achieved before, with fuller depth and in the case of Ball or Pompon dahlias, perfectly globular, and on stems often 2 ft or more in length.

Now you may begin to believe that this minor surgery or disbudding as it is called will affect the seasonal performance of the dahlia plant. Nothing could be further from the truth. By taking away surplus top growth, you encourage replacement growth lower down in what is now becoming a bush. This new development, serviced by that marvellous root system, will rise very quickly to offer multiples of bloom that will astound you as the season progresses. Remember, it is still July as these first flowers appear, and given a reasonable autumn, this genus will continue to bloom until late October — often into November as it awaits the first frost. Indeed, if you practise this minor disbudding carefully throughout the summer, there is no reason at all why the well-structured plant that you create in this way cannot offer you as many as 100 dahlias from July to the frost. That is, of course, among the varieties generally accepted for this purpose, which means those located in the small and miniature ranges and the pompons. Not unnaturally, they are referred to as cut-flower varieties by the nurseries and any trader will gladly recommend the most popular of these to you. A modicum of success in producing bloom quantity can also be achieved in the larger types — from the medium-flowered upwards, but here something else can happen in your garden that will delight you.

The growing of fine, specimen dahlias appeals to many, and whilst this form of culture is akin to the techniques used by exhibitors in their personal search for perfection (a subject which will be dealt with in a later chapter) the specimen dahlia is truly meant to stand in splendour in your garden, showing off its beauty and, of course, satisfying the gardener who wishes to get the best in quality from

Figure 4.8
Tying in the
Dahlias

Figure 4.9
Liquid Feeding
the Dahlias

his plantings. For those with ambitions in this direction, choose the medium-sized varieties and position them so that their greater height is seen to advantage — say at the back of the border. When the first flower-bearing stems arrive, disbud each one for its full length, leaving just two shoots near the stem base to ensure a follow up. The effect will be to have a few very choice examples, and the buds will be larger and fatter than any you have ever seen before. Each one must then be respected for what it is — a specimen. Insure against disaster by tying them individually to your cane support, and attend to their individual needs by extra feeding. The result will be a spectacular display — with blooms from the medium-size range growing to widths of 8 in. or more and those from the wonderful large or giant group to bloom widths between 10-12 in. Add to this the natural depth of each flower, and in the biggest group you will have dahlias as large as footballs — something that your friends, as well as you, can marvel at.

The additional feeding that is necessary to reach perfection in specimen blooms does not of course confine itself to these alone. All of your plantings can benefit from what is generally termed 'summer feeding'. Nowadays, a wide range of such products is available which can be applied at regular intervals during the summer. Many dahlia growers prefer to water on this extra nutrient directly to the root system, or it may be applied very efficiently with the dahlia as a foliar feed. This means that the same mix is sprayed over the plants and absorbed through the leaves with any surplus, of course, draining onto the soil area and being taken into the plant via the roots. The mixing and application of these liquid summer feeds does, naturally, take a little time — especially the foliar-feed method, and for the gardener in a hurry there is a third way to effectively boost your plants. This takes the form of top dressing the whole plot with a powder or granular fertiliser — again widely available in a multitude of forms. Top dressing simply means scattering the powder or granules onto the surface and allowing nature or your own watering activities to take it in dilute form to the roots.

Hamari Fiesta

Lavender Athalie

(left) Lavender Symbol
(bottom left) Cryfield Bryn
(right) Daleko Venus
(bottom right) White Alvas

New Leader

Rotterdam

Vantage

With the dahlia plot in full flower, you may well feel that you can relax and enjoy the fruits of your labour. Indeed you may, but a few words of advice will not come amiss when considering the cutting of blooms for arrangements in your home or presenting to your admiring friends. Remembering that the dahlia in all its massive petal structure and powerful stems is 95 per cent water, it is essential to cut the flowers from the plant when moisture content is at its highest. This means that the very best time to take dahlia blooms is in the early morning, before the sun has reached them. A cool night will have allowed each one to have replenished moisture lost during the previous day, and be crisp, firm and at its best.

Care of Your Dahlia Blooms

When cutting, take a container of water to the plants, rather than cut them and walk around the garden with them in your arms for several minutes before placing them into deep water. The traditional method of transporting an armful of blooms into the house and then arranging them in a vase can be a disaster with this flower, and cut blooms should never be out of water for longer than is absolutely necessary. The reason for this is that the mainly hollow stems need to be full of water, and if they fail to take up water immediately they will often wilt dramatically, never to recover again.

This special care should be continued in the home. Arrange your dahlias quickly, especially the larger types, and choose a position for the display away from sunlight. Never, for example, place a vase of dahlias in the window of your home or on the top of a television set — the rising heat from the latter is certain to limit their life in the vase to hours rather than days. A cool position in the hall or at the back of your living-room would be perfect, and you will certainly have them that much longer to admire if you take this care.

It would be truthful to say that the dahlia is not the longest-lasting cut-flower, but there is such a wide choice of colour and form and the plant is so productive that short-lived displays in the home are very easily replaced even from the smallest dahlia plot.

As the season wends towards its close, you will find, as so many gardeners have, that the dahlia continues to offer

65

you joy and beauty well into the autumn months. When many other summer floral subjects are either over or well past their best, this flower continues to flourish and to brighten the approaching dark days of winter. And that, after all, is what flower gardening is all about.

CHAPTER 5

Pests and Diseases

Like most floral subjects, the dahlia is open to attack from a comprehensive selection of pests and disease. In a way, it is a double target, because it produces not only a flourishing structure of leaf and stem above ground, but also a fat root or tuber underground that is just as likely to be attacked either in growth or during the winter in store.

Nowadays, however, the existence and the persistence of the dahlia's enemies need not be the problem that it was years ago, because the advent of modern preventive measures has made our task that much easier and, with a few exceptions, most of the predators that find their way into your dahlia plot can be dealt with swiftly and effectively. Gone are the days when things like nicotine were our main defence, and notwithstanding the banning of chemicals such as DDT, the horticultural boffins have produced a range of synthetics that, when used sensibly and regularly, keep the largest dahlia planting free from irritating damage.

Of one thing you can be certain, that if you garden for a full twelve months, then some predator or other is ready to attack. During the early months of the year, when your dahlia activities are confined to the greenhouse or cold-frame, then aphides and slugs can threaten your plants, whilst the late spring and summer sees the latter joined by the thrips family, earwigs, caterpillars and rarer visitors like wasps and ants, to say nothing of pests such as red-spider mites, woodlice and wireworms. Even the winter storage period is not without its problems, and whilst this part of the dahlia year is dominated by the possibility of fungus diseases, it is not unknown for overwintering slugs or other soil pests to attack the tuber flesh or the emerging shoots.

By themselves, most of these pests are controllable, but behind the whole scene lies a disturbing undercurrent — the possibility of disease. Pests and diseases are firmly linked, and the most devastating of all the dahlia illnesses — virus — is spread by the action of sap-sucking insects like greenfly and thrips, which transfer, during their nefarious activities, the infected sap from a diseased plant to the sap stream of a healthy plant, thus giving a chain reaction that if left unchecked can decimate if not destroy your entire stock. It may well seem to the beginner that the whole scene is one of despair, and that gardening is a long battle against insects and their evil companion, disease. This does not have to be so, of course, and if we look at our enemies in isolation, then the situation becomes one in which you are the master.

To help you master it, you have not a few allies. The molluscs, the invidious slugs and snails, can be dealt with efficiently by the use of metaldehyde. The aphides, in any of their colourful disguises — green, black or multi-hued, succumb *en masse* to insecticides based on malathion, HCH (formerly BHC — benzene hexachloride), menazon or pirimiphos — methyl or fungicides that are made from carbendazim or benlate. Such names are of little consequence to the ordinary gardener and are, it is fair to say, better known under their trade names, such as the dramatically titled 'Kil' from Fisons (contains malathion); 'Sybol' from ICI with pirimiphos-methyl; 'Hexyl' from Pan Brittanica Industries (contains three for the price of one, with gamma HCH, derris and thiram). PBI offer benlate in their fungicide, May and Baker weigh in a similar product and Boots Garden Products put carbendazim in their garden fungicide. Similar products are produced as a powder for dusting onto plants, and these come in handy puffer packs that make application a simple matter. For effective coverage with the liquid pesticides, a strong pressure sprayer is necessary, and this should be one of your first purchases if you want a clean and healthy dahlia garden. The sort of sprayer that you use will of course

68

depend on the extent of protection you need. For green-house work a small trigger-operated hand-sprayer is usually sufficient, and for a small planting of up to 50 dahlias, a modern plastic 'pump-up' sprayer is well able to cope. For larger quantities, look to one of those 'knapsack' designed sprayers, which are slung on your shoulder or across your back, leaving your hands free to operate the spray exten-sion. As a refinement to the latter, and with the dense foliage of mid-summer in mind, choose one with twin nozzles that can be angled to cover several plants at one attempt. With the defences to hand, let us look more closely at the enemies and see just how they operate and what is best to combat if not nullify their efforts.

Aphides. There is no doubt that greenfly or blackfly are the most persistent of all the dahlias' predators. They need but little encouragement to infest your plants, and can be

Figure 5.1
Spraying:
Early July

69

seen early in the season and as late as November should we experience an Indian summer. They cluster around the soft, new growth and if left unmolested will suck the life-giving sap and leave the developing stem crippled and useless. They breed at a dramatic rate, and ten can become 10,000 in a matter of days, which is why regular spraying is essential to control them. Their crippling effect on the young growth is not however their biggest threat. This comes from the possibility of disease transference (by moving infected sap from one plant to another, healthy one). You should start spraying very early after planting, and maintain a weekly coverage of your entire plot. In this way, you deny the insects' 'build-up' capabilities their full rein, and eventually you will find that your dahlias are free of their attentions. It is a good idea to defeat any immunity that the aphides might build up to a particular insecticide by ringing the changes. Use, for example, a spray based on malathion early in the season, followed later by one containing HCH or derris. It is no problem for you to switch, but very confusing for the aphides.

Aphides in the greenhouse or coldframe are not a real problem if you spray regularly with the hand sprayer

Figure 5.2
Spraying: Aim
Underneath the
Foliage

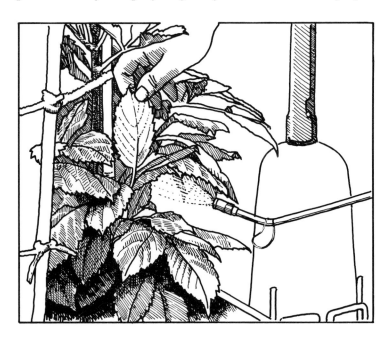

mentioned earlier. It is as well to remember, however, that as the plants — particularly in the coldframe — are usually very close together, that the undersides of broad leaves and the lower parts of thick stems can conceal insects. Aim specifically at these places, and your greenhouse work should soon be free of any unwelcome visitors.

Thrips and Capsid Bugs. Unlike the immobility of the aphides, the thrips family and their larger brethren, the capsid bugs, dart about. This makes them far more difficult to control, and particular attention must be paid to times when they are feeding and to their natural evasive habits. The tiny thrips, in shades of black and brown, are often called thunderflies, and if they get onto the foliage or the opening blooms of your dahlias, then they are unsightly and, worst of all, almost impossible to remove. The larger capsid — brown and green — can do enormous damage, and their sap-sucking activities will badly distort a growing point or flower bud, which will be disfigured by twisted and malformed growth which becomes pitted with small brown holes. They are particularly hard to hit with a contact spray, and are past masters at hiding quickly beneath a leaf or on the opposite side of a stem to the direction of your spray!

The best time to take action against both of these enemies is in the evenings as the sun is setting. They will home in from great distances, and if you spray heavily overhead, and then soak the undersides of your plants, the maximum protection will be obtained. In addition, follow up your dousing of the dahlia plants with a similar treatment of any privet or hawthorn hedge that is in close proximity to your plot. You will be surprised just how many thrips and capsid will have found a home there.

Many dahlia growers find an easier method of dealing with this group — they use a systemic insecticide. Systemic, as the name suggests, implies that the defence is organised from within the plant's system, and this is precisely what it is. The diluted chemical is watered around the dahlia plant or applied as a foliar spray, thus being taken rapidly into the sap stream. The sap becomes toxic, and the theory is that just as soon as a thrips or capsid bug comes along it is killed off at the first bite. My own thoughts on that include some doubts — after all there are tens of thousands of them about, and one bite each is enough to do a great deal of damage. In fairness, however, I have used systemics, but always with the normal 'back-up' of contact spraying. A final reminder — as with the aphides, it is as well to switch your insecticide 'types' during the season to avoid that ever-present possibility of immunity build-up.

Slugs and Snails. One would think that the ponderous movements of slugs and snails would make them an easy target for any defensive measure. That is not always so, and if they are ignored or left to their own devices, then the damage they do at any time of the season can be heart-breaking. I have seen young plants eaten down to the bare stem in a single night, and when the unfortunate owner searched in the morning for the culprits there was not a single one to be found. So much for their lack of speed.

Slugs and snails are mainly nocturnal feeders, and whilst most of us know the pest as the large, fat slug or harmless-looking snail of nursery rhyme fame, it is the smaller, younger slugs that can do most damage. Many of the early hatchings, especially in May and June, are no bigger than a grain of rice — often smaller, and when attacking a dahlia plot in force they can become a real menace, reducing the foliage to tatters. The only real control is by baiting them, or by soaking the soil (in which they hide) with a chemical that they cannot cope with. For some reason, metaldehyde attracts molluscs as aniseed attracts dogs, and once the slug has taken a bite of this chemical it is merely a matter of collecting the victims. The usual method of application is by the use of metaldehyde concealed in compressed bran. They are purchased as slug 'pellets' and the modern types are made showerproof so that they last longer in the open. If you have particularly large infestations, then the chemical can be used, diluted in water, and applied to the affected areas of your dahlia plot. This method is also useful in the greenhouse, when the boxed roots or standing plants can be watered or sprayed with the mixture.

Earwigs, Caterpillars and Other Creepy-crawlies. All these have their day in the dahlia beds, and the worst offender is the earwig. For some unaccountable reason, this darting, devious insect has become associated with the dahlia in a particularly unpleasant way. It is true that the dahlia, with its hollow stems and at times tubular petalling does provide an easy hideaway for the pest, but no more than any other flower. Lupins, delphiniums, chrysanthemums and a host of other floral subjects suffer similarly, and whilst their control is difficult, it is not impossible as many would have us believe. The legend of the earwig's immunity probably stems from its natural defences, because apart from its ability to move very fast and thus avoid your spraying, it also has a hard, shell-like exterior that is difficult to penetrate. Additionally, it has a habit of 'flying' or rather gliding from plant to plant which allows it apparently to disappear as if by magic. To overcome these assets means that you must understand the insect and be devious too.

Firstly, it is mainly a night raider, and so defences should be mounted at that time. Secondly, it has an unchanging habit of seeking dark corners in which to hide during the daytime, so mindful of both these facts, trapping is your best weapon. To do this, place a series of pots, clay ones for preference, on the top of your canes or stakes. After a night feasting on your plants, the earwigs will retreat to the dark interior of these, and it is a simple matter for you to empty the traps every morning into a tin of neat insecticide or paraffin. As an alternative to the pot traps, small pieces of corrugated cardboard, rolled and secured tightly with an elastic band, can be set among the leaves; the effect is the same.

In truth, the earwig is an enigma. Some gardens are overrun with earwigs and others never have any. It breeds rapidly in early June and again in August, and the myriads of tiny nymphs can be of greater nuisance than the parents, especially in the second phase, when opening blooms can be marred by their attentions. You can prevent a lot of this breeding taking place by removing the sort of nesting places that they prefer. Old rustic trellising, for example, with loose bark that the earwigs love, can be stripped clean and creosoted. Long, tufty grass clumps beneath shrubs or bushes is another favourite, and certainly old timber or other bric-à-brac left lying in the garden encourages them to prefer your garden to that of your neighbour. A clean up of these inviting spots is half the battle in the campaign against the earwig. There are many claims from the makers of garden pesticides that their products will also destroy the wily earwig. All I can say is that this has not been my experience. Regular spraying may deter because, after all, who wants to chew a leaf soaked in some unpalatable chemical? But spraying only gets rid of them temporarily; trapping is the surest method of control, and if practised long enough, even the most persistent earwig infestation can be cleared up.

Caterpillars. In a variety of types and colours these can and do feed on your plants in high summer. One of the worst offenders is the one that arrives via the flitting and dancing attentions of the cabbage white butterfly. These butterflies look lovely as they pirouette over the dahlia bed, but with each swoop they find a cosy place to lay a batch of eggs that turn into a mass of crawling green caterpillars. Keen growers control this slow-moving insect by soaking the foliage with a malathion-based insecticide, or by employing a novel, if messy, way of denying the tiny caterpillars access to the essential part of the dahlia plant – the bloom in bud and in flower. This latter precaution involves the use of vaseline (petroleum jelly), which is smeared onto the stems from the last pair of leaves to just below the bud. No caterpillar is able to pass this barrier and if you can bear the sticky mess and the time needed to wipe the stems clean after cutting the blooms, then it is a sure-fire way of protecting your dahlias from an attacker that can mutilate them in seconds, and can render such damage to the partially open bud that it looks like a ragged paper doll when fully open.

Wasps. They may seem an unlikely intruder into your dahlia patch, but intrude they do. Mostly the attacks are confined to a gnawing of the exterior of the hollow stem, and the reason for this unseemly behaviour is twofold:

74

they suck the sugar content of the tissue and also take minute strips of the stem bark for nest-making. The result is a weakening of the stem and in the case of severe attack a wilting of the bloom that it carries. And, of course, the presence of hundreds of wasps crawling over your dahlia bed can be a little unnerving, as they do not hesitate to sring if disturbed in their labours. I have found that normal spraying does not deter them, so traps are set into which they are invited by including some attractive substance that they find more to their liking than the dahlia stem. I prepare small jars of watered beer (half full) or a mix of jam and water, which is sealed with a polythene cover, held in place with an elastic band. A small hole, about the thickness of a pencil is made in the centre, and this opening smeared with some of the prepared substance. The wasps soon find the traps, and their inquisitiveness is their undoing, for they crawl inside to seek the sticky sweetness and eventually drown as they cannot escape through the entrance hole.

Wireworms, Woodlice and Ants. These ground or soil pests can be a nuisance rather than a menace. In a dry summer both ants and woodlice will burrow into and below the dahlia roots, and later in the season, when a tuber is forming, they can and do nest in the fleshier parts, often causing damage. The answer is to see that the soil around the base of the plants is kept moist. This not only keeps these pests at bay, but is of benefit to the well-being of the plant itself. At tuber-lifting time, it may well be that a dry lift, after a prolonged spell of good weather, sees woodlice, particularly, hiding in the tuber crevices to hibernate. If not checked, this means that you take the pests into the greenhouse or winter store, and that can mean trouble. However, the winter store preparations that are discussed in a later chapter should take care of this problem. Some growers have trouble with wireworms, but this is usually on fresh soil, say in new gardens where the turf has been turned in for the first time. Wireworms love this type of loam, and in their travels will bore through the tubers forming underground, often damaging the root system to the obvious disadvantage of the plant. If you suffer the attentions of this pest, you can readily control them with HCH or malathion dustings. A liberal application in the planting holes will usually be sufficient to deter the most adventurous wireworm.

Red Spider. If ever a garden pest was misnamed, then it is the dramatically dubbed red spider. Even the sound of the name sends shivers down the keen gardener's spine. Brought into focus, however, and that is literally true as you need a magnifying glass to spot them, this invader is neither red nor a spider. It is just a tiny mite, almost invisible unless it moves *en masse* and the colour is a muddy brown rather than red. But right name or wrong description, it can attack with such ferocity that a healthy plant can submit to its attentions within a couple of weeks in high summer unless action is taken immediately its presence is spotted. Attacks occur in dry atmospheric conditions, and a hot summer can spark off a floodtide that is very difficult to control once it is established. First sign is a dulling of a normal glowing, healthy leaf, and if the undersides are examined, the clusters of mites will be seen. The speed with which they go about their business is amazing, and if left untouched, the leaves of a dahlia plant will first turn yellow, then brown and eventually the whole bush will succumb. Attacks start near the base of a plant, and regular watering on or near the bottom leaves will help, aided by several good dousings with malathion-based insecticide. Some growers prefer to pick off the dulling or yellowing leaves as soon as they are noticed. This is fine if the pickings are burned immediately. The dahlia is a natural host for the red-spider mite, as the lush summer foliage, interlocking and overlapping, allows a cover and spread for this pest that it delights in. If it is remembered that the undersides of leaves are the points of attack and these are soaked every two or three days, then control can be achieved. Ignore them, however, and they are with you until the rains come.

Diseases and Dahlia Viruses. If insect visitations were not enough, the dahlia, like any other garden subject, is prone to diseases or, worst of all, virus attack. One of the most

Figure 5.3
A Virused Plant

common of the former is dahlia smut sometimes called
dahlia leaf spot or, to give it its grand name — *Entyloma
dahliae*. This is a fungus attack and is almost certainly soil
borne. The spores are carried onto the foliage after heavy
rain has splashed the soil upwards into the plant, and the
first indication that smut has arrived on your plot is the
appearance of small, silvery spots. These turn brown and
the dead tissue eventually falls away, leaving a small, neat
hole. The infection is always from the base upwards, and
the observant grower will note it very quickly and take
remedial action. This means spraying thoroughly with a
good fungicide, based on benlate, a recent addition to our
armoury that is helping to eradicate fungus attacks at
many levels. Smut disease is rarely a hazard to main
flowering, but can be unsightly, of course. Heavy attacks
can be cured by removing the infected foliage and burning
it quickly. Often particular gardens, especially where the
soil is constantly moist and damp, will carry the spores
from season to season, and it needs but a few short, wet
days in summer to start off this nuisance. Once in the soil
it is extremely difficult to clear it completely, but soaking
the soil with fungicide in the spring helps, and growers

pestered with the problem tell me that this does pay off in the end.

Dahlia wilt is another problem altogether because this fungus disease can really cause trouble. The spores usually attack inside the base of a hollow stem, and the first outward sign is a darkening of the stem wall. A push with your finger will indicate a soft interior, and if left unchallenged, this rotting process will travel quickly upwards to deny the bloom life-giving sap and, in the final act, create the wilting of the flower that gives the disease its name. If the main stem is subject to the attentions of this fungus, then the whole plant can collapse in a matter of days. Often your first sight will be a mild drooping of the erstwhile firm, pert foliage, and within hours the whole plant has gone. A dahlia heavily attacked in this way is impossible to restore to full health, and the only answer is to remove it from the bed so that others may survive.

Crown and leafy galls can be worrying, mainly because their appearance is somewhat alarming. Both occur on the tuber that forms underground during the summer and are usually associated with a wet late summer and autumn. Leafy gall is the commoner of the two, and this takes the form of a mass of small shoots that sprout like a cauliflower head from the crown of the root (that is the point where the main stem joins the fattened parts of the developing tuber). These growths just look threatening, even to the experienced, and if propagation is attempted from them then disappointing plants are the result. If you have several roots of the same variety, my advice is to incinerate those affected as soon as they are noticed. If, however, the leafy gall attacks a dahlia tuber that is particularly valuable, then my advice is to pare away or even divide the root, retaining the best and unaffected part for your new stock. If you do this, then almost without exception the growth that starts from the healthy portion does give normal propagating material.

Crown gall offers a similar pattern, except that the disease takes the form of unsightly nodules or bumps rather than leaf growth. These galls appear on the crown — hence the name — and can spread around the full extent of the root rather than confine themselves in one position like the leafy gall. Again, burn the affected stock if you have other healthy tubers, but if it does occur on one that you just have to keep, then take your cuttings from a clean part of the crown, just so long as the shoot is normal and well developed. There is little that you can do to prevent gall attack — many growers never see it at all. However, it happens only to a minute percentage of the dahlia plants and the few tubers that need to be destroyed need cause you no concern. If the problem increases, then the answer is to move your plantings away from the trouble area to a fresh part of the garden.

By far the worst enemy of the dahlia at any level is the incidence of virus disease. Once infected with any of the several viruses that can attack a dahlia plant, there is no cure and the stock must be burned to avoid transmission to the remainder. You may well hear some growers say that a plant will 'grow out of a virus attack'. This is just not true, once infected it is always infected, and even the roots that you would normally overwinter will give rise to virus-infected growth the next season. If a dahlia plant does return to full health after what appears to be a crippling attack, then it means only that it never had virus in the first place, only one or the other symptoms of poor or under-fertilised growth.

The commonest of the dahlia virus diseases that we see in Britain is known as *D. mosaic*, and like all of them, it is transmitted from one plant to another by the movement of infected sap. This movement is brought about by the activities of sap-sucking predators, like the hosts of aphides or the thrips family that flit from plant to plant. A plant that has virus is fairly easy to detect: fortunately, one of the prominent symptoms of *mosaic* is a stunting or dwarfing of the growth. This gives rise to the common name for the affliction — 'Dahlia stunt'. In addition to the obvious distress in the development, virus-infected plants bear telltale yellow markings on the leaf veins, which are also distorted, and on the reverse show a 'blistering' of what would normally be a flat, firm leaf.

Cucumber mosaic virus and *Spotted wilt* are the other forms of this disease that are seen in Britain, although they are rarer than the normal *D. mosaic*. The latter is confined to dahlia plants, but the other can be present in a lot of garden subjects, like cucumber, tomatoes, chrysanthemums, lupins and even garden weeds. Identifying cucumber mosaic is not as easy as for ordinary mosaic, mainly because it does not stunt the plants as dramatically, and often normal growth will occur and just a few telltale markings appear that can be confused with other afflictions. For instance, red spider attack, described earlier in this chapter, gives rise to a belief that virus is present and even the fungus diseases like dahlia wilt are confused with the more serious virus. The leaf markings of cucumber mosaic are noticed because they are a lighter green than the rest of a normal leaf, and occur on any part of a leaf surface rather than follow the leaf veins. Spotted wilt, as the name would suggest, has leaf markings in pronounced spots or as small circles of a much lighter green. The word 'wilt' which appears in the name of this virus is a little misleading, as leaf wilting does not occur as it does with the fungus disease of the same name. It is believed that spotted wilt received its name as a result of the collapse of leaf formations when the virus attacks tomatoes.

The need to destroy infected dahlia plants cannot be over-emphasised. There may be some inconvenience if this has to be done in high summer, but better to leave a few gaps in your display than to have the whole of your stock surrender to virus attack. As has been explained, the transmission of the disease is done by sap-sucking predators, and the obvious defence is a control or elimination of these. Regular spraying programmes are a necessity, and whilst it would be impossible to effect 100 per cent control, constant vigilance can and will reduce the problem to proportions that are acceptable to the amateur grower.

It is fair to comment that a school of thought attributes some of the spread of viruses to other factors, and one of the most popular theories is that infected sap is moved from plant to plant on a knife or blade that is used to take cuttings. This would seem to make the practice of rooting cuttings a less desirable method of propagation than, say, tuber division which requires only that the old root is broken into pieces to form fresh plants. To assume this would be to place the blame on the many thousands of enthusiasts who use the cuttings method, and as this includes a whole international army of dahlia professionals whose livelihood relies on the continued interest that is shown in this flower, their attitude to the virus problem is one that should be looked at critically.

There may be a few miscreants in the trade, and among the large numbers of amateurs who produce thousands of cuttings annually, but in my 30 years of interest in the dahlia I have to say quite emphatically that the dahlia traders are a responsible body, whose concern for firm control of virus diseases is backed up by their very serious attention to the problem that manifests itself in many ways.

For instance, trade societies or associations world wide consult and support the many horticultural organisations, many of them government supported, which are experimenting continually with new methods of virus control and identification, and perhaps most hopeful of all, in ways of producing virus-free stocks which, and this the ultimate goal, remain virus free. Since the dahlia has been in the western world for almost 200 years we might assume that the scientists have failed. The problem is complicated further by factors such as the severity with which it attacks or alternatively the mildness with which it can occur. Often a dahlia plant will have a mild virus attack which acts as a preventative for further, more serious infection — a sort of inoculation. Such plants are, in truth, the worst offenders, because they continue to produce reasonable blooms and yet, beneath the apparent health, lurk stem and leaf that carry the virused sap. Indeed, a fifth column that exists within the dahlia world!

Varieties that have the ability to absorb virus diseases and yet continue to grow normally for any of a number of reasons, like natural immunity or a partial immunisation, are known as 'symptomless carriers'. Several eminent authorities have endeavoured to produce evidence and a blacklist of such varieties, and whilst some even published their findings, many were contradicted or confounded by the continued existence of stocks that were obviously completely healthy. This has given rise to a belief that any dahlia variety which survives without signs of virus for a long time is a natural suspect as being a candidate for the list of symptomless carriers. I would rather believe that there is an elite group of dahlia varieties that are completely immune from virus attack and do not pose the danger in our gardens as do the symptomless carriers.

In all the talk of virus and infection, it would be easy to over-react to the situation and imagine that the problems are insuperable. That is far from the truth. The virus problem cannot be ignored, of course, but it does not dominate all. By far the greatest aspect in all of this is the ability of the dahlia to reproduce itself virus-free from seed. This means that annually massive numbers of new, healthy varieties appear on the world's dahlia markets, and they by far outnumber the virused ones. If we continue to be as watchful as we have always been, and are ever ready to take the simple remedial measures necessary to keep virus attack under control, then the future is assured.

CHAPTER 6

Lifting and Storing

Perhaps the most difficult and even frustrating aspect of dahlia growing experienced by newcomers to this flower is the need, or otherwise, for roots to be lifted in the winter and stored until required the next spring. Before we look at the many and varied ways of achieving successful storing of dahlia tubers, it is advisable to first look at the reasons why we must take them from the soil at all and whether, in truth, we are giving ourselves a lot of extra work each autumn that may not be necessary.

From one or other of the several ways of planting dahlias in late May or June, either as rooted cuttings taken from the overwintered roots, as divisions of the same tuber or, as many growers do, from the whole dahlia root returned annually without disturbance, a cumbersome mass of enlarged root is formed underground which is necessary to use for propagation if the same dahlia is to be grown again in the following year.

When grown from divisions or whole roots, an increase in the original tuber size can be expected, but it is not unusual for a new tuber, formed from the fine roots of a cutting taken in the spring, to be just as large and often more awkwardly shaped than the other types. Most tuber growth takes place between late August and into October, even longer should the weather be agreeable. A warm moist September can give you dahlia tubers of such proportions that the grower wonders if he will ever extricate them from the garden, let alone find room to store them during the winter months. This brings us back to the question of the validity of taking dahlias from the garden each autumn, and whether they might not be better left *in situ* with obviously far less work involved. The answer to the latter point is one that has divided dahlia growers since the species first arrived in Europe, from its subtropical origins, almost 200 years ago. There are many gardeners who will relate to you tales of having left a dahlia root undisturbed for years, and yet it re-appears annually to give another stunning performance. In favoured parts of the country, where winters are less severe than in say Scotland and the north, dahlia roots are left in the soil to overwinter as a regular thing. That the results obtained from this method are equal to those achieved from stock raised from extracted roots is, I venture to suggest, in doubt, as the creation of a new, vigorous root system, provided by rooting cuttings, or by dividing lifted tubers in the spring, is the springboard of quality. In the final analysis, it depends a great deal on your own ambitions; if you are happy with the form and productivity of dahlia blooms produced in the same way as perennials then so be it, but experience has shown that there is no substitute where quality is concerned to the creation of a new and vigorous set of roots. And this is only achieved satisfactorily by taking cuttings or dividing tubers from stock that has been lifted in the autumn.

If we accept that dahlia roots can be left in the soil on occasion throughout the winter months in favoured parts of the country, then it is equally certain that we must accept that the tender tubers have to be lifted elsewhere for reasons other than those posed as labour saving! The large roots that most dahlia varieties produce in the few weeks of summer are soft and vulnerable. They are beloved by a host of winter predators such as slugs, snails and wireworms, who see them as a source of winter food. At any time during the months of scarcity and even as late as May or June, when new growth might emerge, the roots can be savagely attacked by these hungry hordes; and predators are but a part of winter's revenge. Frost is the arch enemy, with fungus attack a close second in terms of destruction. A hard frost, penetrating several inches into the soil, can destroy a dahlia root in minutes, whilst the

Figure 6.1
Lifting Tubers

insidious *botrytis cinerea*, or black rot, will reduce any tuber to pulp even in mild winters. Faced with this, it is fairly apparent why the overwhelming majority of dahlia growers prefer to extract their precious stock and store it away. After all, even if some are lost in store (and that is a fairly common occurrence) the rest fare better than those left to the vagaries of nature.

You can make a start on the autumn dahlia lift as early as October. It is inadvisable however to actually take the tubers from the soil until the end of that month unless you require the area for planting spring bulbs or other subjects. Often you will hear growers talk of needing to have their dahlia plants frosted before they are lifted. Certainly this is a good point, but frosted or not, they can be removed safely from the end of October onwards.

The value of a prior frosting lies in the fact that growth is irrevocably halted, and unless a very mild spell is

85

Figure 6.2
Lifting: Cutting
Back Foliage

experienced the tuber is as large as it will grow and need stay in the soil no longer. Additionally, of course, a fair amount of protection against severe frost attack is afforded to the root by the foliage. Once this has been blackened, that cover has gone and penetration is easier, hence the need to lift reasonably quickly. If you wish to take up your dahlia stock before the first killing frost of winter has struck, then there are a couple of important points to bear in mind. Firstly, a premature lift — say in early October — may result in your root being immature, and unripe tubers have a tendency to shrivel or dehydrate very quickly, especially if they are left exposed to the air on greenhouse staging or the bench of a garden shed. Once this process starts it is very difficult to reverse and the root is destined to be lost. Also, of course, there is the simple time factor; take out a dahlia root a month or six weeks before you need to, and you have that extra length of time to look after it. Like the flower that the tuber has helped produce, once it is severed from its connection with the soil it starts to die. Your job is to keep it in suspension for long enough to put it to the task of creating new plants, and the shorter the period that is needed the more successful you should be.

If you must lift early, and it is readily conceded that so many of us with small gardens need the space if we are to make the plot beautiful in the spring, then prepare yourself fully for the task. Assuming that your daffodil and tulip bulbs need attention and it is early October with no signs of that heavy frost, first pick all the blooms that are available (and there will be many). Next, remove all the ties, canes, stakes and other supports which can be cleaned and stored away for next year. If you are interested in varietal names, *wire* the labels to the base of the main stem or, alternatively, wind a length of coloured wool (consistent with the variety colour) around the stem base so that there will be no confusion when you need them in the spring. Next, cut down that mass of verdant foliage so that you are left with a short stem about 8-10 in. long to which the faithful label or wool clings tenaciously. All the foliage and any other bric-à-brac, like the remainder of the summer mulching material or dead blooms, can be removed to the compost heap, where they will all make a contribution to that invaluable source of soil improver.

You are now ready to take up the tubers, but a word of warning: once you have denuded the plot of foliage and other cover, do not leave the job too long. A snap frost, even in early October, can be strong enough to damage the roots, many of which will be just below the soil surface. It is very difficult to gauge the size or extent of tuber spread from the thickness of the plant stem, so it is advisable to treat each one as if it were big enough to fill your barrow. Indeed, many of them will do just that. The object is to take out the tuber without any damage or at least minimal damage. This is best achieved by using a spade, as a fork can leave a jagged wound on a fat root, where a spade will slice it cleanly should contact be made. This may seem a choice of evils — but a clean cut heals more quickly than one that rips into a root. To get the best lift,

Figure 6.3
A Fork May
Damage Tubers

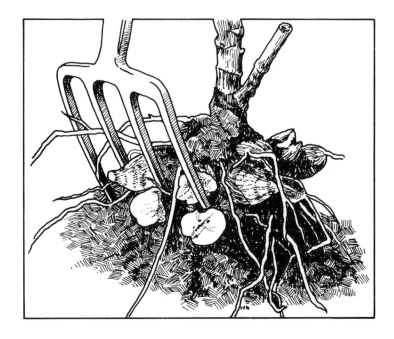

Figure 6.4
Lifting Tubers

88

make an insertion at several points around the stem base —
say a foot or so away on each occasion. By the third
insertion a gentle levering action will see the tuber and
soil rise intact. Place the whole mass, tuber and clinging
soil, on the side of the hole that you have made, and
endeavour to remove as much of your garden as possible
from the intertwining tubers. A short length of cane or a
plant label is ideal for this, but be careful that you do not
damage the tuber skin. It will be impossible to remove all
the soil, but the object at this stage is to get the majority
of it to part company from the root.

With all the roots lifted, take them into your greenhouse
or shed and space them out so that each can receive a full
ration of daylight and, more importantly, be in a position
so that air can circulate freely. Remember that you are
lifting early, so this initial drying process is vital, and if
you are to avoid dehydration, time is important. Too long
on the bench and the telltale signs of shrivelling appear.
After a few days — no longer than three or four — when air
and light have partially dried the roots, the balance of the
soil clinging to the inner tuber 'fingers' can be probed free,
in fact most will fall readily away. You are now ready to
pack the early-lifted roots away, and the aim is to cover
them again in some way to prevent dehydration. To do
this, get boxes made from wood or strong cardboard and
line them with polythene sheeting, deep enough to accommodate the larger tubers. Into the bottom of each container
spread a few inches of dry, granulated peat or clean, dry
soil. Set the tubers onto this base, pushing them together
so that they fit closely, covering the surface fully. It
remains now for you to fill the boxes with the same
plunging material, covering the fattened parts of the root
but leaving the stems clear. Once packed, the boxes can
remain in the greenhouse for a few weeks, until such time
as a permanent winter home can be found for them, which
will be discussed later. What you have achieved at this
stage is a transference of the dahlias from the open garden
into your care under cover. This will give them the best
chance of survival and the chance of loss through dehydration is reduced to a minimum.

The lifting of roots that were left to be frosted in the

Figure 6.5
Trimming Tubers

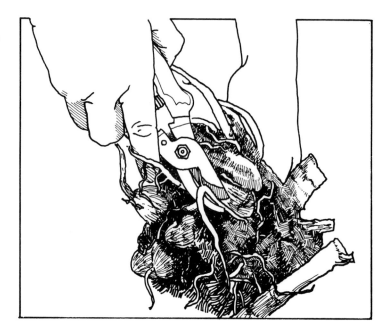

Figure 6.6
Tuber Trimming

garden is very similar, with just a few differences. For example, if you have decided to wait for that frost, then the month of October can be used to advantage. There will be no need to gather all your blooms at one fell swoop, rather you can pick them over the period at your leisure. Similarly, you can take your time in a gradual removal of the canes and stakes, and when the frost strikes, you will be ready to begin operation 'lift'. By the time you have taken up the dahlias it will be mid-November, and whilst you may not have the advantage of sunny days that would have helped to dry the tubers, they will all have put on more weight and will thus be ready for your attention.

However, tubers receiving treatment in November in your greenhouse may well offer other problems for you to solve. There is the question of water content, and in the hollow stems of the larger tubers a dangerous moisture may have been created. To cure this and at the same time assist the drying process before packing begins, cut back that 8 in. long main stem to a mere inch or so. A lot of the water content will disappear when you do this, but to make absolutely sure, core out the main stem, thrusting a thin saw or a screwdriver down the soft, pithy centre so that it emerges through the base of the tuber cluster. The drainage hole that you create means that there is no danger of rot building up, and the sap will dry out within a day or so, leaving a clean, white stem. If you are able to put a little heat in your greenhouse or shed, the drying process for the tubers lifted after frosting will take about ten days. Surplus soil will then be removed easily and you can trim the roots — something not necessary with the early lifted stock. This trimming compacts the root and makes it easy to handle. It is a simple operation, and means only that you remove the thin, hair-like roots that attach themselves to the fatter tubers. An old pair of scissors or even secateurs will do the job effectively, and when you have cleaned away this superfluous root and it is combined with the stem coring, you will have a dry, firm dahlia tuber that will happily go into store equipped to face most conditions.

These preparations may seem unusual, but there is no doubt that the more care that you take then the more likely you are to succeed in carrying the stock safely

Figure 6.7
Cauterising
Tuber Damage

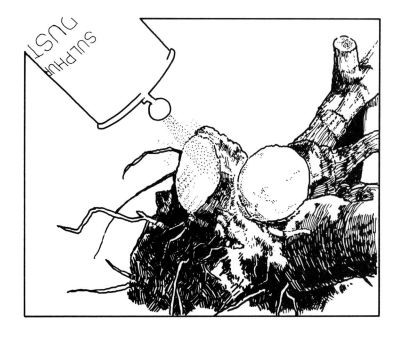

Figure 6.8
Winter Rot

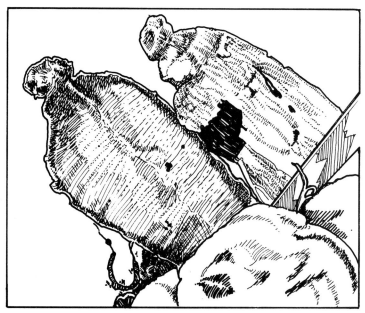

through the winter. And you are not quite finished yet, because once the tuber has been dried and trimmed, you can look for any minor damage that may have been incurred during lifting. A fractured tuber finger that wobbles at the point where it joins the crown should be removed with a clean knife cut, and if you find small wounds or gougings on the tuber itself, do not hesitate to pare back to clean flesh. Any such surgical cuts should be cauterised after they have been made, and you can do this effectively by covering the wound area with flowers of sulphur dust or by dipping the whole root into a benlate solution. This latter fungicide is reasonably new in the dahlia world and has proved very useful indeed in winter protection against fungoidal attack. As an alternative to dipping the whole tuber, the solution can be sprayed over the surface, but whichever method you choose, remember to allow the root to dry out naturally before storing. With your dahlia stock treated in the manner described, you can rest content that you have prepared them efficiently for their winter hibernation. But where to put them for those few, vital months? Firstly it has to be remembered that so many places we might consider to be frost- and damp-proof fail in this particular, and it is not until the first signs of danger show themselves in the most obvious way, with rotting stems or frosted crowns, that we realise our mistake. Wooden sheds or garages without heat are a trap that many fall into. Given normal temperatures they are perfectly all right, but continued mild weather in winter soon produces fungus attack in dahlia roots, and if persistent frost occurs, then it needs just one particularly bad night of plunging temperatures for you to lose your entire stock. The ideal store is one that has a steady temperature level of around 40°F, which is well above freezing point, 32°F, and cool enough to prevent premature growth.

Most greenhouses that are equipped with a modicum of heat, say in the form of soil-warming cables or a thermostatically controlled bar or fan heater, are perfect of course, and where the grower is overwintering other subjects or growing a few low-temperature plants, then the dahlia tubers have a ready-made home. Without a greenhouse, the next best choice is somewhere connected with the house, say a conservatory that is not centrally heated, or a brick-built cupboard or shed attached to the main building. If you have to choose a spot indoors, then you must avoid any room or space that is centrally heated. Even the airing cupboard is a black spot — put your tubers in there and before Christmas they will have been reduced to prunes without a sign of life. One of the places that I was able to store my tubers years ago was a cellar owned by an aunt. It was a chore carting the roots in my car boot backwards and forwards, but the cool cellar, where the temperature was a constant 40°F made the effort worth while. Losses were the lowest that I have ever experienced. Unfortunately that ideal spot is no longer available to me but offers from friends have included a church building with walls several feet thick (perfect) and a loft over a builder's yard that was ideally suited for storing anything, let alone my stock of dahlias! If personal good fortune plays a part in the storage spot that you can select, then the reverse applies to the methods of packing the roots away. I have never believed that you can just leave tubers unprotected or uncovered, and some measure of any success achieved, I am firmly convinced, can be attributed to sensible packing. As described for the dahlia tubers that have to be lifted early, the boxing in peat or soil is a preventative against shrivelling or dehydration. There is no reason to believe that because a root is somewhat larger in girth and a little maturer, that it does not also need cover. It is, for example, a common practice in the dahlia trade to lift tubers in say November, and after some preparatory trimming and cleaning, bench them in the greenhouse in peat or moist leaf-mould. Heat is kept low until growth is required, and then the heat factor is increased and moisture given to start the roots into growth. There is a lesson to be learned for the amateur here, and whilst it is not usually necessary for most gardeners to begin propagation in January (the month chosen by the professionals), the theory that covered roots keep better is surely confirmed.

Packing trimmed roots is a pleasant and easy matter. I have used tomato trays with those useful short legs that permit several to be stacked one upon another. Peat or dry

Figure 6.9
Tubers Trimmed
and Ready
to Store

soil, vermiculite or straw, even shredded paper can be used to bed the roots, and the shortened stems allow you to place the stock neatly into position so that the next box fits into place above it. In this way, a tomato tray will take six to eight average-sized roots, which means that you can accommodate a great many in a very small space. This, after all, is the object of the whole exercise: cleanliness and compactness, allied with firm packing. And yet another plus is given by this method, that of ease of access for examination, because one thing that must be maintained during the winter months is a watch on the roots. What could be easier than lifting each tray down from time to time and scanning the displayed contents for damage or fungus attack?

So far in this discourse on lifting and storing roots I have covered the accepted practices, that is, those that have been used by the majority of dahlia lovers for years and, naturally, have the best track record in terms of stock survival. There are, of course, many other ways in which dahlia tubers can be stored. Some may seem bizarre, others perhaps suit your particular circumstances. Take, for example, the netting of roots. This storage method entails the use of ordinary garden netting, often used to support rows of peas or beans. A length of the netting is laid out, and covered to a depth of several inches with clean, dry straw. A row of tubers, stems shortened as I have already described, is placed down the centre of the package, which is then rolled into a 'sausage' and secured at the ends and in the centre with twine. This protected package can then be stored almost anywhere, or even, as I have seen on occasions, hung from the rafters like a prime ham. Similar parcels of roots, again using straw, can be made with discarded tights — and it is surprising just how many tubers will pack into those. They may look a little odd suspended from say the garage roof, but it is an effective method of storage.

Another method that has made its appearance in recent years is the use of black plastic bags. To exclude light, it is advisable to obtain black or dark coloured bags, and they should be strong, not the very flimsy types that are used by councils for rubbish collection. The tubers can be packed into the bag and they must be dry. The secret is to then seal the bag tightly, using thin garden wire wound around the neck several times. You might be forgiven for believing that condensation would form and harm the roots. If the bag is denied air then it does not harm the contents, and provided that the bags are located in that frost- and damp-proof store, then they will survive until you need them.

So far we have discussed the storing of tubers produced in an average garden — say anything from 20 to 100 roots. There are many who grow more than this, and they have a method which is very time-saving and efficient. It is, of course, clamping, a term well known in agriculture, where the clamping of such products as potatoes is still one of the best ways of keeping vegetative material in a healthy state. Dahlia tubers respond very well to this treatment, and if you have a lot of stock, then dig a hole in your garden that will be large enough to hold it all. Choose a spot beneath a tree or high shrub as the roots will offer a natural drainage system. Cover the bottom of the pit with a foot or so of dry straw, lining the sides similarly. Now bed the roots tightly into the straw-filled hole, and cover

Polyand

Doc van Horn

Abridge Taffy

Go American

Pink Willo

Super

Salmon Symbol

Kung Fu

Connoisseur's Choice

King Soccer

Opal

the last layer with a further foot of straw. You can now replace the excavated soil, forming it into a rounded or sloped mound. Many growers leave the clamp like this, but I prefer a double sheet of heavy-gauge polythene placed over the whole structure, which is held firm against the winter winds with heavy stones or piled earth. Some of my friends even rope the polythene into place, pegging it on four sides. The result is a cosy store that is certainly frost-proof and apart from occasional visitations from a few wandering mice or the odd mollusc attack, the roots are safe until needed. The clamp does, however, have one disadvantage — once open you cannot safely re-seal it, which means that it is best left closed until such time as you are ready to use all the roots that have been stored there.

Lifting, and more particularly storing, of dahlia roots is not an easy gardening chore — but it is one that, given careful attention, can give the gardener a great deal of pleasure. After all, if you do manage to get a lot of happy, healthy roots through the dark days of winter, it pays off not only in terms of satisfaction, but in hard cash as well.

CHAPTER 7

Exhibiting

The world of dahlia exhibiting is divided into two parts: one inhabited by the professionals and an entirely different world peopled by dedicated enthusiasts whose rules and standards are self-imposed. The professional displays and exhibiting techniques are well known. Who has not seen the towering dahlia spectaculars at leading horticultural shows like Southport and Shrewsbury? And even the world's greatest flower show — the Royal Horticultural Society's Chelsea show — is often graced by the dahlia, albeit two months before nature intended that this versatile flower should bloom in the scheme of things.

In this chapter I intend to deal with the world of the amateur showman and the manner by which the exquisite exhibits are created and how they are divided one from another when facing the critical eyes of the judge. I called the amateur dahlia show scene a 'different' world with self-imposed rules. That is no understatement, because most of the devotees who involve themselves in this fascinating hobby are prepared to go to the greatest pains and expense to produce winning exhibits during the peak period — early August to late September, when flower shows abound nationwide. It would be fair to comment that hardly any one of that vast number of horticultural shows excludes the dahlia from its schedule of classes, whether it is the smallest village horticultural society show or one of the major exhibitions, like those at Southport and Shrewsbury. I called the standards and rules that the dahlia showman revels in 'self-imposed', and that is exactly what they are. The gardener looking at his dahlias in high summer might well believe that they were exquisite and grown to their full potential. The showman would probably have other ideas! There can be no personal likes or dislikes in the show world, the standards and the rules are set rigidly by Britain's supreme authority, the National Dahlia Society, and its 1,200 affiliated societies follow this criteria closely, both in the wording of their schedules and in the adjudication of the classes. That there are debates, disagreements, even some animosity, about the rules would not be denied, but they are framed democratically and criticised in a similar manner. Changes are made from time to time, but by and large they are peripheral and the basic concept of a good exhibition dahlia is undeniably set. In a way, this creates what can only be described as artificial standards, because beauty always being in the eye of the beholder, the detailed perfections must, of necessity, be the view of only the small inner group of experts who framed them originally and whose successors maintain them to this day. But then we all live by the rules (or we should!) and the flowerman can not be an exception. From the many conferences and meetings that I have attended over the last 30 years, I know that the present rules have evolved through democratic debate. Long may it remain so.

Having touched upon the dahlia's exhibition standards in general, let us look at them in particular: as you will have read in Chapter 2, there are ten dahlia groupings, and each of these, with certain overlaps, are considered for exhibition. Three of these groups, namely the *Decorative*, *Cactus* and *Semi-Cactus* are sub-divided into five separate sizes ranging from giants through large flowered, mediums, small flowered to the smallest grouping, the miniatures. A further group, the *Ball* group, is divided into two sizes, the so-called *small Balls* and the *miniature Balls*. One other group, the *Pompon*, has an imposed size limit also.

These sizings and sub-divisions are important, because with one exception (the giant types), classified varieties are subject to disqualification, and if you enter blooms at a show and exceed the imposed size limits, then your exhibit would be disqualified. So the first thing that the showman must learn is to grow his dahlias within the limits, otherwise he is wasting his time. These are the disqualification sizes that the National Dahlia Society imposes:

Giants	Can be grown to any size
Large	Must not exceed 260 mm (10.25 in.)
Medium	Must not exceed 220 mm (8.75 in.)
Smalls	Must not exceed 170 mm (6.75 in.)
Miniatures	Must not exceed 115 mm (4.5 in.)
Pompons	Must not exceed 52 mm (2 in.)

To implement these disqualification rules for oversize, the National Dahlia Society has produced a set of measuring rings, and the delicate placing of these over each bloom in a dahlia exhibit is one of the fascinating, if bizarre, features of the judge's routine. Mostly unseen by the public (who are excluded when the judges are going their rounds) the 'ringing' of dahlias has been, perhaps, the most controversial of all the many dahlia rulings. I recall recently attending a conference of the French Dahlia Society in St Quentin, and being invited to judge at the show that was held in conjunction with the conference. Naturally, as an Englishman abroad, I produced my judging rings. My Gallic contemporaries fell about in disbelief, and I could only explain that we measure flowers because, well — because we are English!

Size of an exhibition dahlia may well, in the eyes of many enthusiasts, have complicated the hobby if not inhibited it, but it is in truth only one of several pitfalls for the showman that can end in disqualification. For example, it is an offence to support a bloom (say with wire or other material) above the level of the vase that is holding it, a rule that was highlighted when it was discovered that wires were being used internally to keep recalcitrant stems upright. How you can trace a wire inside a flower stem is still a mystery to many. However, the National Dahlia Society is very firm on this point, and it has ruled that if a showman is discovered flaunting the regulation, he can, after due examination, be banned from exhibiting for a year.

Other disqualification rules are more mundane: if you

100

enter a dahlia in a class other than that for which its form is a requisite (for example a cactus type in the decorative classes) then it will be ruled out. Similarly, if the schedule calls for five blooms in a vase (and buds are classed as blooms in this context) and six blooms have been entered, then this entry would also receive a marking on the card 'N.A.S.', which is the judge's cryptic way of telling the entrant that his vase is 'Not According to Schedule'.

If you manage to survive the initial disqualifications, it is then, and only then, that the judge will look at your entry with interest. Even at this point, the official will have strict guidelines to follow and these are known as the dahlias' 'ideals'. Every bloom is judged against perfection, and as there is no such thing as the perfect dahlia, the blooms lose points for each flaw. It is a sound basis, of course, and has stood the test of time. Every bloom that was ever grown has a fault. It may be so minuscule that it would not be seen by most, but the judge's job is to find it or its multiples, and thus divide the exhibits into first, second and third place. In my experience there has never been a draw in dahlia exhibiting, and that alone is evidence that the system works.

The faults that the judge can find are many. Imperfections are graded into very serious faults, and those of lesser degree. Amongst the former are such things as malformation (a distortion of the normal symmetry or outline of the flower), blooms that face downwards (pendant on the stem), bad damage (bruising, insect bites, etc.), wilting (a drooping of a petal or group of petals), evidence of 'doctoring' (removal of damaged petals to improve the condition of the exhibit), open or 'daisy-eye' centre (where a double bloom opens to reveal the middle), green centres (a bad one this, where green bracts mix with the central petals to form a hard, green middle), petal gapping (missing florets in the outline with consequent disfigurement) and even formational difference, whereby a cactus form tends, for example, to decorative petalling. Lesser faults include: oval or sunken centres; irregular or oval outline of a dahlia; uneven, irregular or unbalanced form; petals lacking freshness, and petals that are bleached, discoloured, faded, bruised or even eaten by those predators I have talked about in a previous chapter. Uneven tipping on bicoloured blooms is also a fault, as are shallow blooms (lack of depth from the front to the rear), dahlias that are not mature, or conversely, those that are past their best and, of course, the presence of insects, such as aphides (greenfly and blackfly), is also on the fault list.

You can see from all of this that the judge has a real task in sorting out the wheat from the chaff, and if he is to be at all successful and please even a proportion of the showmen whose exhibits he is judging, then he must know what a good dahlia looks like in the first place. Here the instructions, again created by the National Dahlia Society, are very specific. The main exhibition groups, the decoratives, cactus and semi-cactus types, must be double flowered (a closed centre), symmetrical in all respects with a perfectly circular outline. The centre must be proportionate to the rest of the flower with the depth at least two-thirds that of the diameter. The bloom must be poised at an angle of not less than 45° to the stem which should be straight and of a length and thickness proportionate to the size of the bloom. All the other exhibition types have similar instructions, with slight variations according to their particular form, but with this base on which to set his target, the judge must come to a rational decision setting fault against perfection.

That there are some 400 judges nationwide on the Society's list says something for the persistence and loyalty of this élite group, because within the world of dahlia showmen there is little lack of knowledge, and indeed many exhibitors are themselves judges. It might well be asked why the National Dahlia Society has never devised a 'points' system of judging dahlias, which surely could have few critics. The truth is that one facet of dahlia judging does include a points scheme. This applies to multi-vase classes which, in the main, occur only at major and specialist shows. And even here, judges are not compelled to use the points system, they are merely offered as a guidance for this complicated specialist type of dahlia exhibit.

This latter supplement to the judging rules is relatively new, and even now is under fire from some exhibitors. It would appear that the awarding of points can cause a greater divergence of opinion than that caused by the detraction of ideals, and whilst judging by numbers (as it is called) happens in many other countries such as the United States of America, it has never found favour with the British dahlia enthusiast. From all of this you could be forgiven for believing that dahlia exhibiting was a virtual minefield, and that aspiring showmen would be deterred by it all. Many have said that the dahlia is the most complicated flower to sort out on the show bench, and when you consider the many flower-show judges, like parks' directors, administrators etc., are asked to reach decisions against this background of complex rules, then the opinion would seem to be a valid one. It is on this aspect that many dahlia enthusiasts agree wholeheartedly, and if interest in the art of exhibiting is to flourish, then some simplification of the present rules would seem overdue.

Creating Dahlias that Win Prizes

Exhibiting rules apart, the showman still has to produce blooms that win those elegant silver trophies or the magical 'red card', a hallmark of success. Fortunately, this is not nearly as complicated as it might appear, and the fact that many thousands of gardeners do so every summer would seem evidence enough. And the small British army of devotees is not alone – in South Africa, Canada, America, Australia, and New Zealand, similar shows for the amateur exhibitor abound, and each country mentioned has its national organisation that sets the rules. Naturally, these vary somewhat, but a tightening up of international classifications in the 1960s created a dahlia language that is understood universally. Indeed, the situation is such that, with very few exceptions, the best dahlias raised in those countries fulfil the ideals of a good show dahlia in Britain, with the reverse also applying. Perhaps the most encouraging thing about this is the very fine line that exists between dahlias grown for garden or cut-flower pleasure and those grown especially for show work. Many varieties are capable of filling several roles, and it is the few extra tasks required that make a dahlia fit for the exhibition bench as opposed to living out its life in a vase on your sideboard.

These differences, if differences they are, can be categorised as follows: selection, restriction, individual attention, and protection. Selection means that you must grow the varieties that naturally achieve the ideals of perfection mentioned above; restriction is best described as a control of the plant, to ensure that no excess foliage or bloom is carried; individual attention means concentration on each and every flower you grow and protection extends to covering your dahlia area if necessary to make certain that the end product is not damaged by excessive sun or beating rain. Taking these four points separately, selection may seem an obvious one, but failure to grow the right dahlia varieties means you would never have a chance of winning top prizes. The types that win prizes do change from season to season, but not that dramatically. Many of the top winners have been grown for 15 years or more and these are always contained in dahlia prize-winning analyses printed in the gardening press or in the literature issued by the National Dahlia Society. Contrary to popular belief, the 'classic dahlias' as they are called in the hobby are relatively inexpensive and you will find many of them listed in Chapter 8. Naturally the dahlia enthusiast likes to try something new in order to gain a head start over his rivals, and this element of experimentation and enterprise pays off for some, although for others it can be an expensive exercise as novelties are never cheap.

If you are contemplating starting a collection, then start with those that have a good record of success, and combine this with the conditions you have to contend with in your own garden and under your particular method of cultivation. A light soil, for example, will give results on one variety that make it unbeatable — transfer the same variety to another garden where the soil is heavy and climatic conditions vary, and you will have a disaster. Trial and error are the keywords, and only you can find out what does well for you. Oddly enough, this is one of the factors that attracts so many newcomers to dahlia exhibiting, because even showmen of long experience will readily admit that a complete beginner can, in his very first year of competition, produce blooms that match or even outstrip theirs.

The operative point is a simple one: start with the right varieties and your battle for success is half won. Restriction or the elimination of unwanted leaf and bloom in your exhibition plants is one that is widely accepted by showmen. Regrettably, there is little room for compromise in this, as a dahlia plant left to its own devices with no limitation on the quantity of flower that it produces will give you second-class exhibition blooms, and that is not the object. The reason for the removal of excess on every plant is to channel all the energies that the root system produces into a limited number of dahlias. If you are aiming to grow show-worthy giants, for example, then it is a matter of simple mathematics that six flowers grown on one plant are just not going to be as big and as effective as three. Not that biggest is always best, but depth of bloom (discussed earlier), stem strength and those all-important size factors come into this, and they will never happen if your plant is allowed to languish unchecked. The aim is to create a structured plant, with each bloom catered for.

To do this means stopping all of your plants very early in the season. This procedure is a removal of the main or leading growth point which gives you immediate control over the flower-bearing stems that then start to develop from each leaf axil lower down on each plant. Say that there are five pairs of leaves sprouting from a young dahlia. By the middle of June, in the case of most types, the growth centre must be cut or snapped away thus leaving you ten possible stem laterals, as the flower stems are called. The number of laterals that you leave in position will govern the future quality, so that, in the case of those giants we mentioned, you must leave only three of the ten to eventually flower. Drastic? Yes it is, and many growers blanch at the thought of this pruning that denies them a bloom mass. But as I said earlier, sentiment must play no part, and if you want to compete then just three, or at the most four, of those laterals must survive. The others are removed gradually — say one or two every week, until by the middle of July just three strong stems are growing lustily. It is then that you will see the value of de-lateralling — the term used for this operation. Each of your chosen branches will be powerfully constructed, and a fat bud

105

will emerge which just breathes that it is going to be a winner. You are not, however, finished just yet — the three favoured stems will each endeavour to thwart your efforts by producing side shoots of their own. When the main bud forms at the top of each, a further couple of ancillary shoots will appear immediately below, and in every lower leaf axil small shoots will start to emerge. All of these must also be removed, and this is the final disbudding that will leave you with a clear run to that truly big dahlia. It is widely accepted in the world of dahlia exhibiting that the first 'flush' of bloom is the best. This means that you will have just three flowers from this particular giant and you have to make each one count. It is easy to see why show-men grow a lot of plants when they set out to compete at many shows. They know that you cannot grow a lot of top dahlias on just a few plants, so they reverse the procedure and grow a few blooms on a lot of plants.

The de-lateralling and disbudding that I have described for the giant-flowered varieties apply throughout the whole size range with the exception of the poms. In the large section, for example, five or six laterals are left to bloom; the mediums, with a top exhibition limit of 8.75 in., will carry six to eight blooms; the small flowered will carry eight to ten, with the miniatures carrying from ten to twelve. These figures are general for the average garden, and naturally can vary if your conditions or soil are better (or worse, of course). So far as the poms are concerned, they have a different problem. You will recall earlier in this chapter I talked about disqualification — well at 52 mm (2 in.) this tiny dahlia is very likely to go oversize if restricted. This means that in the case of most exhibition pompons no de-lateralling or dis-budding must take place and they are allowed to grow naturally. With all types, the maxim that the first bloom (or 'flush') is best must be maintained, although there are differences, albeit small. For example, the poms that I have mentioned going oversize, can be corrected in this habit by the appearance of the second flush or crop of flowers. Similarly, the miniatures and smalls can be coaxed to produce winning blooms off the second flush — but it is advisable to restrict the number of side shoots and heavily disbud if the quality is to be constant throughout the show season. A major part of a dahlia showman's skill is to maintain top quality, and whilst certain standards can be obtained from a single plant, the best approach, and that adopted by top exhibitors, is to control all the first flushes by staggered planting.

Staggered exhibition planting or a phasing of the times that your best blooms appear — remembering the two-month spread of the shows — is achieved very simply. Plants at varying stages of development are set out in late May, running through even to the end of June (for the very late shows). This is one of the major reasons why showmen prefer plants for exhibition as opposed to tubers or divisions, as the time that the plants are rooted (through April to May) relates to their development, and it is far easier to select on this basis than on the somewhat erratic growth of tubers. With many exhibition flowers, there is talk of timing the arrival of the best blooms — even to a particular day! The dahlia is not quite as obliging as this, and whilst a spread target date of say two weeks can be achieved in most seasons, so much is dependent on the vagaries of our summer weather that luck plays a big part in all of this. The dahlia showman's annual cry when the shows come around is either — 'I am too late' or 'I am too early' — never, it seems are they ever on time!

Whenever and wherever dahlia exhibiting is discussed, the subject of extra feeding crops up. It is commonly believed that the dahlia needs to wallow in fertiliser if it is ever to win prizes — this is far from the truth. Naturally a certain level of fertility has to be maintained, but bearing in mind those disqualification sizes, any excess application of feed, whether it is organic or inorganic, can be harmful. That not only applies to the sizes, it has a bearing on the quality of the dahlias that are produced. Nitrogen is very necessary for steady growth, but if too much is applied, then the flowers produced are soft, thus encouraging wilting; form is also distorted (and that factor is paramount these days) and lastly colour is dramatically affected. You might well think that red is red and nothing can change that. Give a red dahlia too much nitrogen, and it fades into a muddy brown soon spotted by the discerning judge. The purple, pink, lilac and orange shades can also suffer from colour deficiency if overfed.

Having warned against excess feeding, that is not to say that you should ignore feeding altogether. If the soil in which exhibition dahlias are grown is prepared correctly during the previous autumn and winter as described in Chapter 4, then summer feeding can be carried out as dictated by both seasonal growth and weather conditions. A wet summer, for example, will unlock a lot more nitrogen from your soil than will a dry one and the early plants will be lush, strong in the stem and bursting with energy. Add more nitrogenous feed to a situation like that, and you will induce soft growth as well as all those problems of wilting and colour deficiency. A prolonged warm spell, on the other hand, will see the plants somewhat backward, and this will need to be remedied by keeping the plot moist and adding fortnightly feeds either in the form of diluted liquid fertiliser or as a foliar spray — both methods described in Chapter 4.

Exhibition plants are always best played by ear — which means that most of it is a matter of trial and error and, of course, experience. What is good for one planting of show dahlias might not be good for another only 20 miles away! Most importantly, endeavour to treat your plants as individuals rather than as one large group. Your poms may be languishing, whilst your giants are romping away — to feed them all the same thing at the same time will cause the one to be corrected and the other to over-react. Study the needs of the different types you are growing and feed or water them as their needs demand.

This question of treating your show blooms as individuals also extends to the necessary support and protection. If we do restrict a plant, then the extra energy allocated to a smaller number of stems means that they might not be satisfied with a general tying in of an entire bush, which can lead to distorted growth and a curving or malformation of the stem. Add extra canes or stakes to hold the stronger growing blooms, and in the case of the giants or large-flowered varieties, perhaps a cane to each one.

Protection is also of great importance if you are to win prizes. The word is one that most gardeners associate with the normal routines of hygiene, and a campaign that must be carried out regularly to keep the plants free from insect damage. This must be done as a matter of course, but in the wider interpretation of the word from the showman's viewpoint, it means covering the growing dahlias to prevent damage from scorching sun or from beating rain. Show blooms can be grown without protection of this sort admittedly, but the dahlia world is divided on the need for some form of cover over exhibition flowers. My view is that the giants and large types, and even the top-level displays of medium-flowered dahlias, would never achieve the perfection that they do without covering. Many leading showmen erect polythene or glass structures over their entire plot, with heights of 8-10 ft that give a fair clearance above the tallest growing variety. Others are less ambitious, and provide smaller covers, with the favourite being the popular cones. These conical covers are made from heavy-gauge polythene or roofing felt, and their construction is a pleasant job for the dark days of winter. A circle, 2 ft in diameter is cut from the material, and a small wedge cut to the centre. The cone can then be formed by rolling towards the middle, and secured with staples or glue. A wire ring holds the base of the circle firm, and this is held with wire clips. If the material is clear, then it should be coated with white emulsion paint to exclude glare. To hold the cones in the most favoured position requires the addition of three or four long canes, which are held at angles to the wire ring, meeting in the centre (at the apex) very much like a foreshortened Indian tepee. With these 'legs', it will be seen that you can move the cone around your garden to cover any bloom, in any position and at an adjustable height. The advantage that cones offer is that they are mobile, light to handle and can be stored away for the winter. The complete plot cover may be more efficient with its unquestioned greater coverage, but it must still be lived with throughout the winter months, unless it is constructed from portable roofing and removable support posts, as are many modern structures.

Covering a dahlia plot, even partially, may not be everybody's choice, but it helps unquestionably to win prizes in the area of giant and large blooms. Lower down the size scale I can offer some consolation to those who rebel at the idea of turning their garden into a mass of wood and polythene. Many champion growers who specialise in the small-flowered, miniature and pompon groups have never placed a cover over any of their blooms. They maintain, and with indisputable evidence, that the additional tasks involved (apart from construction) such as extra watering of the plants (because, under cover, your dahlias are denied nature's gifts) and the higher temperatures that polythene or glass create, are hazards they can well do without. It seems, you make your choice and live by it.

Perhaps the greatest hurdle that the aspiring showman faces is one that has little to do with the constant battles against insects or the swaying ocean of leaf and bloom that seeks your attention, but with the movement of your show blooms from their position in the garden to a point on the showbench, perhaps some 50 miles away. A dahlia can look a gilt-edged winner as it sways gently in the evening breeze in the back garden, but without some special care and know-how, that same bloom can become an also-ran when vased up to face the critical eye of the judge.

Cutting, packing, transport and staging are just as important as cultivation, and there are many showmen who freely admit that whilst they can produce a pristine dahlia on the bush, it is a different matter when it comes to cutting and staging. Cutting may sound a simple procedure, but do it incorrectly or at the wrong time, and your precious bloom can be lost. As said before, the best time to take a dahlia from the plant is first thing in the morning, when it is full of sap and offers most resistance to wilting. Never cut a bloom in full sun or if it is for show, any time during the daytime, sunny or no. Always take a container of water to the plant rather than walk around the garden with an armful of dahlias. Cut well into the bush just above the strongest following shoot and at an angle of 45°. This angled cut means that the hollow stem will not 'bottom' on either the container or vase, which might well inhibit the entry of life-giving water during its short cut-life. If you have blooms of the large sizes to get to the show, that it is advisable to tape or tie a thin cane to their entire stem-lengths, thus limiting the amount of sway that can occur even on the best conducted journey.

To move blooms from home to show may require some special equipment, and showmen have a variety of devices to achieve this. Favourite is the wooden carrying case; constructed of light materials it is large enough to hold the biggest flower you will grow, and has a series of internal bars, against which the caned stem is fastened. The stem end is inserted into a small water container, and some even use balloons, filled with that life-giving liquid, which are placed over the end of each dahlia. Others use small plastic containers or tubes, with lightness being the main consideration. Not so involved is the carrying tub. This is a large metal container that will hold a foot or so of water and can carry safely some dozen blooms. If small holes are bored around the rim, the stems can be held with padded ties at this point, thus holding the cargo securely on the longest journey.

If you intend making one or other of these carrying devices, remember to take into consideration the height of the vehicle you will be using. It is no good setting a certain height and then finding that it is a foot too much! Naturally, the exhibitor with a lot of blooms to transport will need something like a small van, as the family saloon, with some exceptions of course, is usually too small for this job. At any of the country's specialist shows, you can see a fleet of hire vans and even, for the larger operators, a furniture van packed to the gunwales with blooms.

On arrival at the show, it is advisable to select a quiet corner for the important job of staging your exhibits. There are many things to remember — complete your entry cards; name the exhibits; obtain and fill your vases and, last hurdle at which many fall, put the correct number of blooms in your vase and ensure it is in the correct class.

Now comes the final act in the showman's calendar — arranging the blooms in a vase or vases so that the judge will select yours rather than those of your rival. Staging, in the scheme of exhibiting, would appear to have little or no value. The National Dahlia Society's rules ask only that staging is neat and tidy and the Society instructs its judges to take this into consideration only when, and I quote, 'All other things are equal'. In practice, however, dahlia exhibit-staging is far more important than that. A badly staged vase of blooms with the edge on another exhibit, which is slightly inferior in quality yet has been well staged, might well lose the verdict just because of the arrangement. A bent stem, for example, can be disguised by angling it the way that it curves rather than the reverse. A bloom angle, a fault if it differs from others in the vase, can be adjusted by placing it higher or lower in the set. Misshapen centres can be gently squeezed to a better shape, and even blooms that lack depth can be cajoled into an appearance of this necessary quality if stroked persistently for a few minutes! All of this comes under the heading of staging and showmanship.

If you are setting up three blooms in a vase, the standard 'pyramid' staging is best — that is one bloom set above the other two to form an equidistant triangle. Five blooms can follow the 'W' formation, with three dahlias staged neatly above the other two. Make all your blooms look squarely at the judge and space them geometrically apart. A few minutes spent adjusting the exhibit can well make the difference between a first and second award. Finally, colour — perhaps the dahlia's grandest asset: always make the very best of this, and match for a balance of shades if you are showing blooms of differing varieties together. If the exhibit is one that contains dahlias of the same variety and colour, ensure that the colours match perfectly.

It has always been my experience that dahlia-show people are the friendliest in the world. There is never any dearth of guidance for the beginner or even willing helpers when you are struggling to finish your exhibit in time for the judges. Indeed, that is how many of them, if not all of them, were introduced into the hobby, by friendly encounter and an exchange of information. Many of my compatriots nation wide never see one another from one show season to the next, but when they meet they greet each other like brothers and sisters. Naturally, they all like to win — the spirit of competition is such that it could not be otherwise. But that they could be accused of being inward-looking or even secretive is a charge that would have them bellowing with laughter. Dahlia exhibiting for many is a way of life — and a very pleasant way of life at that.

CHAPTER 8

A Selection of Varieties

There is little doubt that the dahlia offers the gardener a wider choice of variety than any other genus. Allowing for the vast difference in sizes, the form variance and a permutation of colour that excludes only the blue shades, it is easy to understand why the official Royal Horticultural Society's listing contains some 20,000 names. But that is only a tip of this floral iceberg — many tens of thousands of dahlia varieties never reach the lofty heights of official recognition, and languish in nurseries and gardens unknown just waiting to be discovered.

Even to attempt a selection that would suit every purpose is somewhat daunting and so in opening just a small corner of this treasure chest, I would commend that the reader seeks his own ideal of beauty. To make the reference easy, a code is used to indicate the recommended uses for my selections. The codes are as follows:

(S) = Suitable for the showman
(CF) = Ideal for cut-flower or general garden use
(B) = Useful for bedding schemes
(FA) = For floral artwork or home arrangements

Single-flowered Varieties

Bambino (B & FA) — tiny blooms, 1 in. wide in white and yellow blends.
Coltness Gem (B) — can be raised from seed in all shades

except that elusive blue.

Exotic Dwarf (B & FA) — officially called 'lilliputs' there are many colours in this group of minuscule dahlias. This one is pink.

Nellie Geerlings (B & FA) — red with a bright-yellow 'eye'. A beauty.

Omo (B & FA) — white, as the name suggests.

Princess Marie Jose (B) — a lilac bedder from Holland.

Red Dwarf (B & FA) — a bright-red lilliput, which makes a good subject for pot or tub culture on a patio or balcony.

Yellow Hammer (B) — a favourite of parks' and gardens' superintendents. Yellow, strong growing and prolific.

Anemone-flowered Dahlias

Shaped like the flower after which they are named, this form is one of the rare types, with just a few varieties in commerce.

Comet (FA) — this Australian import is dark red, and has been a favourite for many years, with its central clutch of tubular petals.

Honey (B) — pink and yellow blends with a low-growing habit.

Scarlet Comet (FA) — a bright scarlet sport of *Comet*.

Collerette Dahlias

Single flowered, with a central ring (the collar) of shorter petals. Most grow around 3 ft in height.

Can-Can (S, CF & FA) — this trial-awarded lilac with white collar is highly adaptable.

Chimborazo (S) — bright red and yellow, this is one of the present exhibition favourites.

Choh (B) — the only listed lilliput collerette. Purple and white it comes from Japan and the word means butterfly.

Clair de Lune (S & CF) — all yellow shades, it is a strong grower with sturdy stems for cutting.

Easter Sunday (CF & FA) — an elegant collerette that is all white.

Gigolo (S) — flame red and white — popular with exhibitors.

La Cierva (S & CF) — purple-tipped white, with white collar, yet another that wins prizes on the showbench.

Mariposa (S & CF) — a personal favourite this, in lilac pink and white.

Sunburst (S & CF) — fairly new, it is an eye-catching combination of scarlet and yellow. ′

Thais (S) — multi-hued in red, purple and white — excellent variety for exhibition.

Giant-flowered Decorative Dahlias

Massive blooms, many growing over 1 ft in diameter. Chiefly the darlings of the exhibitor, there is always that sense of achievement if you grow them well for your own pleasure.

Almand's Climax (S) — lilac and white, a top show winner from the USA.

Alvas Supreme (S) — perhaps the most successful giant of recent years, this New Zealand yellow is strong growing with excellent form.

Cherokee Beauty (S) — a massive pink, low growing, from USA.

Croydon Masterpiece (S) — from Australia, the colour is described as burnt sienna, or shall we say dark bronze. A show favourite of many years' standing.

Evelyn Rumbold (S) — a rich, royal purple that wins prizes readily.

Go American (S) — like several other top giants, from the USA. Bronze blends shaping into winning form.

Hamari Girl (S) — probably the finest giant decorative raised in Britain. A pink that lends itself to the beginner.

Holland Festival (S) — there are not many bicoloured giants, but this orange-tipped white from Holland is amongst the best.

Jocondo (S) — Holland raised this purple beauty that is grown, almost without exception, by the lovers of this type.

Kidd's Climax (S) — a mix of pink, white and yellow give this New Zealand beauty an exotic look. One of the best giants in cultivation today.

Lavengro (S) — lavender shades with some bronze, this British-raised beauty is another that is very easy to grow to perfection.

Liberator (S) — sometimes called 'Pop Harris', it is a rich red formal giant from Australia.

Lula Pattie (S) — a tremendous white from America — possibly the biggest variety we have. A little informal on occasions.

Night Editor (S) — the geometric perfection of the royal-purple winner from America makes it a personal favourite.

Playboy (S) — One of the best giant decoratives of recent years, a British raising which has achieved international fame on the showbench.

The Master (S) — a bronze from Australia that has maintained favouritism with showmen for two decades.

White Alvas (S) — a white sport of famous *Alvas Supreme*, it is very new. With the same form as the parent, this British dahlia is assured of a successful future.

Large-flowered Decorative Dahlias

Slightly smaller than the giants, the large group settle around the 8-10 in. mark, and tend to be more formal than their larger brothers. Most have excellent stems, and whilst hardly suitable for cut-flower work, do make a gracious addition to your garden if grown simply for display. For the purpose of this selection list, however, they are graded as for exhibition only.

Bedford Sally (S) — not British as the name suggests, but from the USA (Bedford, Ohio). A recent arrival with great promise.

Ed Lloyd (S) — a strong-growing dark pink on good stems.

Enfield Salmon (S) — another with a deceptive name. It comes from Enfield in Australia and is a dark pink. Very popular with exhibitors.

117

Inca Metropolitan (S) — British raised, a very formal yellow on strong stems. One for the beginner.

Mrs McDonald Quill (S) — almost a legend, this red-tipped white from New Zealand is a firm favourite with dahlia lovers everywhere.

Polyand (S) — no doubting that this lavender pink from Australia is the most popular large decorative in Britain, as well as overseas.

Shirley Jane (S) — bronze and yellow combine in this beauty from the USA. Another leading contender on the showbench.

Silver City (S) — a British-raised white of immaculate form. It still wins prizes regularly although some 20 years old.

Medium-flowered Decorative Dahlias

With bloom widths between 6-8 in., this middle of the road group offers fine exhibition dahlias as well as many that can be used for cut-flower work.

Alloway Cottage (S) — yellow with some pink overtones, a New Zealand variety that has found favour with British growers.

Daleko National (S) — a British medium decorative in lilac shades. Good form for show and with powerful stems.

Dana Louise (S) — a recent arrival in pure white, this one is British-raised and is establishing a fine reputation.

Duet (S) — deep blood-red with even white tips makes this import from the USA both attractive and needed for show work.

Edna C. (S) — a sensation when it arrived from the USA several years ago, it is still one of the best yellows for exhibition.

Evelyn Foster (S) — a white that took the showbench by storm. From the USA, is one of our top varieties.

First Lady (S) — a third American medium with reflexing formation in bright yellow. Another favourite.

Gilt Edge (S & CF) — pink, edged gold (hence the name), it is excellent for exhibiting and is included as cut-flower because of its beautiful colouring.

House of Orange (CF) — brilliant orange medium from

Holland. Outdated for show work, but in a vase —
stupendous!

Inca Matchless (S) — yellow shades in a geometrically
perfect medium.

King Soccer (S) — purely for the showman, this strongly
built medium from Holland is not the easiest to grow to
perfection. When achieved, it is a winner.

Purple Joy (S) — a new arrival from Australia, the rich
purple hues and neat form have already given it showbench success.

Red Sensation (S) — British raised, this trophy winner fills
a colour need within this group.

Rustig (S) — South Africa gave us this yellow medium.
Strong plants bear show-winning blooms all season.

Terpo (S & CF) — this bright-red Dutch variety was the
rage a decade ago — now it makes only rare appearances
on the showbench, but can still please best in the
garden.

Small-flowered Decorative Dahlias

It is in this group, with bloom widths between 4-6 in., that
many cut-flower dahlias overlap with those suited also for
exhibition. Called 'dual-purpose' varieties, they straddle
the narrow line between blooms suitable for showing and
those that you can cut plentifully.

Angora (CF & FA) — a white, fimbriated variety (split-
petalled) that looks like a carnation. Very elegant in
arrangements.

Arabian Knight (CF) — as near black as you will get. In
truth a red, of course, but one of the rarer colours.

Buttercrunch (CF & FA) — with a name like this you can
expect, and get, a lovely dahlia. Yellow blends for this
British beauty.

Disneyland (CF) — another where the name betrays.
Yellow, red and bronze shades blend in this attractive
small decorative.

Edinburgh (CF) — a true oldie that has stood the test of
time, chiefly because of its rich purple, tipped white
hues.

Frank Hornsey (S & CF) — orange and yellow, this is the father of many sports — pink, yellow, pearl and rose in colour. All are worthy of your attention for show or the garden.

Gerrie Hoek (CF & FA) — this Dutch variety is probably the best-known in the world of dahlias. The pink blooms have the popular 'water-lily' form and grow ceaselessly from July to October.

Glorie van Heemstede (CF & FA) — almost as famous as *Gerrie Hoek* this sister variety in the same form is pale yellow.

Hamari Fiesta (CF) — scarlet with butter yellow, this is one of our most popular garden dahlias. British raised, it is sold every spring in tens of thousands.

John Street (CF & FA) — a red water-lily dahlia of recent introduction and will be as popular as 'Gerrie Hoek' when better known.

Kung Fu (S) — a bright red, well-shaped, strong-stemmed, small-flowered decorative that will win you prizes.

Lady Linda (S & CF) — pale yellow faintly tipped with lavender, this is one of the successes of recent years. Ideal for exhibition and equally at home as a variety for cutting.

Nunton Harvest (S) — orange bronze, with a formal petal make-up, this long-stemmed British raising is best suited for show work.

Porcelain (CF & FA) — the name suggests the colour — white and lilac blends — very elegant. A water-lily shaped variety.

Rothesay Robin (S) — dark pink, this Scottish dahlia has an equally handsome sport named *Pink Robin*. Both are highly rated by showmen.

Rutland (CF) — purple with overtones, this is a personal favourite. Cutting from July to the frosts, it is invaluable for the gardener with limited space.

Scarlet Beauty (CF) — Holland gave us this red water-lily cut-flower. Matches well with *Gerrie Hoek* or *Glorie van Heemstede*.

Twiggy (CF & FA) — long and slender stems (as the name suggests) for this pink small in that popular water-lily form.

Wootton Carol (S) — soft pink and white with reflexing petalling make this a choice for the showman.

Worton Ruth (S & CF) — pink, purple and bronze combine in this attractive dahlia that is suitable for exhibition and cut-flower work.

Miniature-flowered Decorative Dahlias

The miniatures grow up to 4 in. in diameter, and this means usually that you can expect more blooms per plant. Most of the miniatures, therefore, can be used for cut-flower or garden culture, with the best shaped being the favourites of exhibitors.

Abridge Taffy (S) — a white show miniature of merit. British raised, it is of recent introduction.

Anthony Pellant (CF) — a purple of prolific habit. Another newcomer that will become a cut-flower favourite.

Chorus Girl (CF & FA) — you will probably have seen this pink in your florist's shop. A very widely grown cut-flower.

David Howard (B, CF & FA) — rich orange with contrasting dark, bronzy foliage, this is one of the widely known dahlias. Good for bedding as well as filling your vases.

Dr John Grainger (S) — an orange bronze show miniature in the decorative group.

Jean Fairs (CF & FA) — orange and bronze for this floral art favourite that cuts at any stage — in bud or fully out.

Jo's Choice (S) — showmen love this red and grow it by the thousand every summer. A ready-made winner.

Mistill Delight (S, CF & FA) — white with lavender blush, this Cumbrian dahlia is truly a dahlia for all purposes.

Newby (S & CF) — grown well, this pink-blended beauty has the form to win. Fail for show work, and you have the perfect cut-flower.

Small Ball Dahlias

This section is the direct descendant of the Victorian Double Show and Fancy types. Our forefathers loved the globular form of this group, and raised them by the thousand. Today we have a more limited choice, but the tight petalling still make them a favourite with many gardeners.

Alltami Cherry (S & CF) — a bright red from Wales, that has the form for exhibition work as well as for your vases.

Alltami Supreme (S & CF) — a virtual replica of Alltami Cherry, but in a rich, butter yellow.

Bonny Blue (CF) — sometimes called *Blue Danube*, this is one of the oldest and most popular Ball dahlias we have. Not blue, of course, but rich lavender for this venerable veteran.

Charles Dickens (S) — a Dutch origination in light pink to purple, best role would seem to be that of a showman's flower.

Crichton Honey (S & CF) — colour as name, and this northern dahlia (from Co. Durham) can be used for show or cut-flower.

Highgate Robbie (S) — a powerfully built bloom in darkest red. Might startle in a vase on your sideboard, but is best on the showbench.

Opal (S & CF) — Australian in shades of opal. Has won thousands of prizes world wide, and yet can still be happily cut for the home.

Risca Miner (S) — a new purple of excellent show form. Not Welsh as the name would indicate, but raised in East Anglia.

Rokesley Rocket (S) — a bright red, with form that exhibitors love. A recent raising from North London.

Vaguely Noble (S) — named after a thoroughbred, this is also a first-rate dahlia. It has a pink spot named *Pink Vaguely Noble* that will be as successful on the show-bench as is its parent.

Miniature Ball Dahlias

The miniature Balls are slightly smaller in diameter than the Small Balls, with widths that average 3-4 in. The compactness and geometric petal finish is more pronounced, simply because they are smaller.

Cherida (CF & FA) — a mix of lavender and buff, this is a fine addition to any collection that looks for plenty of bloom for arrangements.

Chic (S) — rich, violet purple in this raising from Holland. It has seen successful service on the showbench for many years.

Connoisseur's Choice (S & CF) — brilliant flame red, this Dutch beauty has been winning prizes and filling vases for years now.

Downham Royal (S & CF) — royal purple that is, perhaps, the top winner at exhibitions from this group. Cuts beautifully to match your other lighter shades.

Nellie Birch (CF) — a former show favourite now relegated to cut-flower work where it has lost none of its charm. Very dark red.

Nettie (S & CF) — yellow, this is a firm favourite with showmen and will also give you some very handsome blooms for your arrangements.

Pride of Berlin (CF) — lavender pink, is often called *Stolze von Berlin* and can be seen in garden centres and supermarkets every spring. A very popular cut-flower.

Rothesay Superb (S & CF) — this bright-red dahlia from Scotland is a universal favourite for exhibition and garden use. A long-standing reputation for reliability.

Valerie Buller (S) — a rich, dark red, this is a showman's dahlia and has already started a winning career on its recent maiden appearance.

Wootton Cupid (S & CF) — various shades of pink combine to make this little beauty a winner at any level. British raised in Warwickshire.

Worton Joy (S & CF) — a lavender pink on good, strong stems. Will show early and late in the season as well as double for cut-flower work.

Pompon Dahlias

Small and compact, no more than 2 in. in diameter, these are the *true* pompons, not to be confused with the so-called

'Dutch poms' that include miniature Balls and miniature decoratives. Fine for all purposes, i.e. show, cut-flower or floral artwork, they are just about everyone's favourites.

Andrew Lockwood (S) – a lilac that is best at home on the showbench, although a fair supply of cut blooms is always available.

Czar Willo (CF) – I have seen this purple on the show-bench, but it is better suited for the provision of elegant little blooms for your vases.

Diana Gregory (S) – an Australian, in lavender and white that has an enviable reputation stretching back for years. Most showmen grow this.

Don's Diana (S) – a purple sport of the lovely *Diana Gregory*. British raised, it is another exhibition favourite.

Frank Holmes (S, CF) – lilac and white, as so many poms in variation are, this recent arrival from Australia is a beauty.

Golden Willo (S) – a corn-coloured favourite of mine. You can win prizes with this one and cut the extra blooms for your vase.

Grand Willo (S) – the name 'Willo' as a prefix or suffix with the pompons denotes they are Australian from famous raiser Norman Williams. This lilac is well up to his acknowledged standards.

Hallmark (S & CF) – pink, and one of the best poms in cultivation today. Show it, cut it or leave it in splendour in your garden.

Iris (S) – a red, almost purple, gown for *Iris*. It has the shape to win and does so with regularity.

Mark Lockwood (S & CF) – a perfectly formed lilac pom that is at home on the showbench and can give you masses of perfect cut blooms.

Moor Place (S) – a long-standing exhibitor's pom, and perhaps the most widely grown and shown. A deep, rich purple.

Noreen (S & CF) – a blend of pink and purple make this one different. The form is perfect for show work.

Rhonda (S & CF) – one of our oldest poms – and not from Wales, but from Australia. Lilac and white, is known world wide and wins regularly.

Small World (S & CF) – one of the few white poms, and a

good one. Sometimes has a reddish fleck on the petals.

Sue Willo (S & CF) — another Australian as so many winners are — purple with that winning perfect globularity.

William John (S) — I like this robust pom in shades of orange and red. Wins prizes but varies somewhat in colour in a changing season.

Willo's Night (S) — almost black, and with such beautiful form that it is a regular in pom grower's gardens every summer.

Willo's Violet (S & CF) — a personal favourite, in attractive violet hues. It still wins regularly, although a true veteran these days.

Cactus-flowered Dahlias

The true cactus-flowered dahlias have long, pointed petals that are rolled almost throughout their entire length. This 'spiky' or star shape gives the attraction and a reason why so many enthusiasts love this group.

Giant-flowered Cactus Dahlias

Polar Sight (S) — this is a rare group, simply because very few raisers interest themselves in breeding the very big sizes. *Polar Sight*, a white from Holland, is one that has stood the test of time.

Yvonne Marie (S) — this lavender pink is British raised, and of recent introduction. It could be a good addition to this sparse section.

Large-flowered Cactus Dahlias

Light Music (S) — lilac blends for this tall-growing, strong-stemmed winner from Holland. Has made friends world wide.

Paul Critchley (S) — a dark pink of excellent form that has been awarded several times. British raised.

Pride of Holland (S) — another dark pink with an ambitious name that it deserves. A fine dahlia.

125

Medium-flowered Cactus Dahlias

Arthur Lashlie (S & CF) — a bright red that has its fair share of prizes and offers plenty to the cut-flower enthusiast.

Banker (S) — flame red, this Dutch introduction has sharp petals that make it formationally perfect for show work.

Caroussel (CF) — a rich purple with petals that incurve dramatically. An unusual dahlia that is widely grown for its colour.

Galator (S & CF) — this orange to red cactus has sports in yellow and gold (*Yellow Galator* and *Golden Galator*). They are a reliable dahlia family and come highly recommended.

Sure Thing (S & CF) — a scarlet beauty for all purposes from Holland.

Wake Up! (CF) — another personal favourite — the bright-red petals and sharp form are delightful in any garden.

Small-flowered Cactus Dahlias

This group, with blooms between 4-6 in. in diameter is another that offers every service. Show varieties abound, and there are just as many that will offer cut blooms from July until November.

Alvas Doris (S & CF) — a bright-red New Zealander that has won trophies and other awards world wide. A dahlia for all purposes.

Athalie (S) — a dark pink that already has a sport (*Lavender Athalie*). This is a showman's dream, as will be the lavender sport.

Border Princess (B) — there are several 'Border' prefixed varieties in varying colours. This one is orange and yellow and a beauty.

Cryfield Max (S) — a difficult one to get to perfection, but when that is done, it is a sure-fire winner. A light yellow.

Diorette (S & CF) — another pale yellow, this time from Holland. Of excellent form and offering plenty of extra bloom for your arrangements.

Doris Day (CF) — a dahlia name of fame! Scarlet cut-flower, it also has a purple sport cannily named *Doris*

Knight.

Earl Marc (S) — a newcomer, finely petalled for exhibition in white to lilac. A sparse grower.

Higherfield Crown (S) — a breezy yellow of recent introduction that is already making a name for itself on the showbench.

Klankstad Kerkrade (S & CF) — one of the dahlias of all time. Highly awarded all over the world, it has topped our exhibition charts on many occasions. Grow this one, because it will do everything for you. It was raised in Holland and is a pale, sulphur yellow. It has two sports, *Majestic Kerkrade*, a pink and yellow, and *White Kerkrade*. Both emulate their parent.

Monk Marc (S) — strictly a show dahlia in my book, although others like the rich pink hues. Low growing with excellent form.

Park Princess (B) — from Holland, this low-growing bedder will give you the greatest pleasure. It is a personal favourite.

Miniature-flowered Cactus Dahlias

The miniature cactus is another very sparsely populated section. There is no apparent reason for this, as the varieties that we have are excellent, and make first-rate cut-flower or even exhibition subjects.

Frank Soeten (B) — a white double-flowered bedder with a wide reputation for reliability. Low growing and long flowering.

Little Glenfern (S & CF) — an Australian variety of recent introduction. An exquisitely formed miniature in yellow that wins prizes as well as giving you armfuls of blooms throughout the summer.

Rokesley Mini (S & CF) — a white of excellent quality. Plenty of bloom in that attractive 'spiky' form, with exhibition-worthy flowers regularly produced.

127

Semi-cactus Flowered Dahlias

The semi-cactus forms are halfway between the decorative petalling and the pure cactus. They are extremely popular with showmen, because their full-petalled blooms give the necessary 'depth' that wins prizes. They are, however, equally capable of producing masses of cut blooms for the average gardener intent just on growing excellent varieties.

Giant-flowered Semi-cactus Dahlias

Alfred C. (S) — orange to bronze for this massive variety from California. A recent arrival, it is being grown with success by all the top showmen in the section.

Bedford Mary (S) — another new arrival from the USA, in yellow. Strong grower on powerful stems.

Daleko Jupiter (S) — a really big giant semi-cactus in red and yellow shades that has a form beloved of the giant grower. A recent release, it has already won many top awards.

Daleko Polonia (S) — orange and yellow, this is another, earlier release from the same raiser as *Jupiter*. A showman's favourite.

Gateway (S) — this Dutch raising is one of the best white giants we have.

Hamari Dream (S) — British, yellow and a long-standing favourite. Has a habit of shedding petals when near maturity.

Inca Dambuster (S) — perhaps the largest dahlia raised in Britain. It can be grown to 14 in. in diameter quite easily. Pale yellow, it has swept the world since its arrival a few years ago and now flourishes in the USA and the Antipodes.

Real Delight (S) — a soft salmon, this Dutch favourite attains excellent show form and so is widely grown by top showmen.

Respectable (S) — this orange/yellow blend reigned supreme in the fifties and sixties, and still wins prizes 20 years later! Not as powerful as it was, but still a force to be reckoned with.

Super (S) — a mid-red, the form cannot be faulted. Stems

are straight and strong, making it a top variety in the showman's book.

Surprise (S) — pink with some yellow at base, this American dahlia used to be one of the biggest we had. Not so today, although it can still spring a surprise when well grown!

Vantage (S) — a yellow, it is one that came along to usurp *Surprise*. Again from the United States, it has good form if not pushed too hard.

Large-flowered Semi-cactus Dahlias

Buoyance (S) — a mix of orange and bronze, this elegantly formed LSC is a showman's standby. Dutch raised and early to bloom.

De Sarasate (S) — a glowing red large semi-cactus from Holland, it has stems like ramrods and grows fiercely all season long.

Doc van Horn (S) — in shades of pink, this last raising from famous Dutch raiser Dirk Maarse is one of his best. A ready-made show winner and one that the beginner can tackle.

Hamari Princess (S) — the beautiful blend of soft yellow touched lavender pink make this a garden eye-catcher as well as a top show dahlia.

Nantenan (S) — the dahlia that shaped a thousand others! This famous Dutch raising has been the yardstick by which many hundreds of others have been judged. A veteran but still capable of top successes.

Neveric (S) — a bright orange with some yellow, this Yorkshire-raised introduction of the late seventies has had plenty of success.

Reginald Keene (S) — the famous 'Reginald', an orange/ bronze winner, now has two sports of equal quality, *Candy Keene* (pink) and *Salmon Keene* (light pink). A great show family to own.

Wootton Hotspur (S) — a new British large semi-cactus in bright red.

Medium-flowered Semi-cactus Dahlias

Amelisweerd (S) — a pale-bronze medium from Holland that attains perfect form for exhibition. It is often difficult to overwinter.

Carnaval (CF) — a bright red and gold oldie that is beloved by thousands. Cut and vased, it is spectacular. No wonder it is so popular!

Daleko Venus (S) — a lovely blend of lavender and white and with a form to please the showman. A fine new arrival.

Davenport Sunlight (S & CF) — this is another newcomer of merit. Yellow as the name suggests, it has elegant form and cuts for vasing too.

Eastwood Moonlight (S) — Moonlight and Sunlight — what lovely names. Another top show winner in pale yellow.

Evita (S) — a deeper yellow winner of recent introduction. British raised.

Golden Heart (CF) — this legendary dahlia has been loved for 30 years. Scarlet with a gold centre, it will bewitch you.

Hamari Bride (S) — snow white, the form is first rate and has given this show dahlia an enviable reputation.

Highgate Torch (S & CF) — flame red, this medium semi-cactus won the Wisley Trial grounds highest award in 1980 — a First Class Certificate for all round perform-ance — show and garden.

Rotterdam (S & CF) — thirty years old and still going strong! Will still give show blooms if well treated and is ideal for cutting. A mid-red.

Suffolk Bride (S) — with *Hamari Bride* is one of the best two whites we have.

Symbol (S) — this Dutch raising, a generation old — has taken every award the dahlia world has to offer. A bronze, it has a family of sports in salmon, pink, rose and yellow that almost corner the show market in this group. 'Symbol' is a classical dahlia, you could do no better than grow it and its family.

Topmost (S) — white flushing to a delicate pink make this a most attractive dahlia. Its forte, however, is on the showbench.

Small-flowered Semi-cactus Dahlias

Cheerio (CF & FA) — bright cherry-red with silver tips make this the cut-flower favourite. Australian, it is an eye-catching beauty.

Cryfield Bryn (S) — this is strictly a show dahlia — immaculate form and habit make it so. Health has been a problem, but clean stock makes it almost unbeatable. British raised, it is bright yellow.

Downham (B) — this yellow double bedder has been grown by parks authorities for years. I cannot conceive what they would do without it.

Hoek's Yellow (CF & FA) — another favourite for cut-flower. From Holland it is grown in its tens of thousands every summer.

Kiwi Brother (S) — another strictly for the showman — pink and bronze blends — a most unusual combination. Excellent form.

Margie (S & CF) — orange, it is good for show and cuts well. There is also a pink sport (*Pink Margie*) that is as good as the parent.

Match (CF & FA) — this South African dahlia in clear white, tipped purple, is one of the best floral art varieties we have. The colours are dramatic and lend themselves to many forms of arrangement.

Vidal Tracy (S) — a lovely pink-blended dahlia of recent introduction. Strictly for show although the colours might appeal to some.

Wootton Wedding (S & CF) — white as driven snow — a beauty for any purpose and highly productive.

Miniature-flowered Semi-cactus Dahlias

Andrie's Orange (B & CF) — bright orange, and known internationally as a very reliable cutter. Also useful for bedding in mid-border.

Ella's Snip (CF) — a dark pink that produces masses of blooms.

Lynne Bartholomew (S & CF) — a purple miniature with delicate form that is good enough to win prizes. Excellent also for cut-flowers.

131

Snip (S & CF) — orange bronze, a neatly formed bloom allows it to be shown on occasions, although it is better for cutting.

Miscellaneous Dahlias

This group contains a number of unusual petal forms and other types that do not fall into the normal petal patterns. Many of these are very useful for floral artwork or other home arrangements by virtue of their individuality.

Giraffe (CF & FA) — the yellow and bronze of this dahlia, which has the form of a double-flowered orchid, resemble the colours of the giraffe. Thin, wiry stems make it very adaptable. There is also a pink sport named, not surprisingly, *Pink Giraffe.*

Jescot Julie (CF & FA) — orange-faced petals have a purple reverse on this strap-petalled newcomer. A very different form, and a pleasing addition to the dahlia's repertoire.

Mickey Mouse (B & CF) — this semi-double, light-pink dahlia is low growing and suitable, therefore, for bedding. Tiny blooms on thin stems allow cutting for miniature arrangements.

Tiny Tot (B & FA) — another fascinating little dahlia. Pink shades and low growth made it adaptable for tub or pot planting on a patio, bedding out or for floral artwork.

White Orchid (CF & FA) — sometimes called *Weisse Orchidee*, this white dahlia has the form of a single-flowered orchid. Very attractive and decidedly different.

If you wish to know more about varieties or keep up to date with the changing scene in the dahlia world, then the literature issued free to members of the National Dahlia Society would be of great value.

You can become a member by writing to the General Secretary, 26 Burns Road, Lillington, Leamington, Warwickshire, CV32 7ER. Currently, the annual subscription is £4.68, which includes VAT and postage. There are reduced subscription rates for members over 65 years of age and special facilities for joint membership (man and wife).

List of Recommended Suppliers

BRITAIN

Aylett Nurseries Ltd., North Orbital Road (A.405), St Albans, Herts (Telephone: 0727 22255). All types available, and specialising in cut-flower and floral art types. Excellent show garden open to the public during flowering time.

Braintris Dahlia Nursery, Beccles, Suffolk, NR34 7RL (Telephone: 0502 715728 or 715489). Well known for supplying exhibition varieties in plant or tuber form, but also carries an excellent list of garden types.

Halls of Heddon, West Heddon Nurseries, Heddon on the Wall, Newcastle upon Tyne, NE15 0JS (Telephone: 06614 2445). An extensive modern list annually augmented with novelties. Supplies tubers and plants for all purposes.

Scotland's Dahlia Centre, Dunshelt Nurseries, Ladybank Road, Dunshelt, Auchtermuchty, Fife (Telephone: Auchtermuchty 274). Tubers and plants obtainable here, from a strong list containing varieties suitable for garden and exhibition. The nursery is the scene of the Scottish National C & D Society's annual dahlia trials — visitors very welcome.

Butterfields Dahlia Nursery, Harvest Hill, Upper Bourne End, Bucks (Telephone: 06285 25455). Some rare groups obtainable here, like 'Topmix' and 'collerettes'. Tubers or plants and a warm welcome at flowering time to interested societies or individuals.

Oscroft's Dahlias, Sprotborough Road, Doncaster, Yorkshire (Telephone: 0302 785026). A very extensive list with many novelties, tubers or plants and, like several of the other suppliers, offers collections of either at reduced prices.

Gilbert G. Titchard (Dahlias), Meadowsweet Nursery, Uppingham, Rutland, Leicestershire, LE15 9TU (Telephone: Uppingham 2451). Plants or tubers, and a fine selection including many with the accent on colour difference raised at the nursery.

L. Staite & Sons Ltd., Avon Nurseries, Evesham, Worcestershire (Telephone: Evesham 6212). Beautiful nurseries near the river Avon. Bulk supplies of plants a speciality, which might well interest large groups or societies.

Samuel Dobie & Son Ltd., Upper Dee Mills, Llangollen, Clwyd, LL20 8SD (Telephone: 0978 860119). Tubers available in most forms, including some for flower arrangers and for dwarf bedding use. They also have a comprehensive list of seed dahlias.

Suttons Ltd., Hele Road, Torquay, Devon, TQ2 7QJ (Telephone: 0803 62011). A colourful list of tubers available from cactus and decoratives to poms. Seeds also a speciality, with several types not available elsewhere.

ON THE CONTINENT

Bloemisterij G. Aartsen, Vlierburgweg 25, 3847 RJ, Harderwijk, Holland (Telephone: 03410 12089). An excellent list of dahlias with an international flavour. Tubers of varieties from Germany, Belgium and France as well as Holland. Nursery is open to visitors at flowering time.

Lindhout Ornata, Speciale Dahliaculturen, Herenweg 105, 2201 AE, Noordwijk, Holland (Telephone: 01719 15567). Very competitive tuber prices, and a fine list of international raisings including many Dutch trials winners. Open in September and October to visitors, who are made very welcome.

C. Geerlings (Dahlien Culturen), Kadijk 38, 2104 AA,

Heemstede, Holland (no telephone number available). A beautiful nursery on the outskirts of elegant Heemstede, that welcomes visitors. Tubers available in most types, with a very good list of collerettes, many raised at the nursery.

Hugo Vallaeys, Dahlia Nurseries, Poperinghe, Belgium (no telephone number). The leading dahlia trader in Belgium, with many awards from shows all over Europe. A very comprehensive list including some lovely cactus types of their own raising. Visitors very welcome.

***You can correspond in English with the four continental nurserymen mentioned above, and they can converse very knowledgeably with visitors.

UNITED STATES

Stanley Johnson, Pennypack Dahlias, Cheltenham, Pennsylvania 19012, USA. A renowned American trader, with a special interest in giant dahlias. Tubers only, of course, sold between December and March.

Comstock Dahlia Gardens, PO Box 608, Solana Beach, California 92075, USA. Tubers of all types available from this nursery in the Californian sun. One speciality: sun-ripened dahlia seed that many enthusiasts find exciting to grow.

White Dahlia Gardens, 2480 S.E. Creighton Ave., Milwaukee, Oregon 97222, USA. A firm that has been in business for almost 70 years. Tubers and seed available.

Phil Traff Dahlias, 1316 — 132nd Avenue East, Sumner, Washington 98390, USA. A relatively new trader in the States with a first-class list of international varieties, many imported from Europe, Japan and Australia. Tubers available December/March.

The Blue Dahlia Gardens, San Jose, Illinois 62682, USA. Ken Furrer's Blue Dahlia Gardens are known all over the world and with good reason. His list is massive, and he travels widely to add to it each year. Tubers and seed available.

Almand's Dahlia Gardens, 2541 W.Avenue 133, San Leandro, California 94577, USA. Jack Almand is another leading American dahlia trader, and is famous for his own raisings, many of which are internationally famous. Tubers or seeds available.

***It is best to write for catalogues from American nurserymen (in the first instance). Tubers are usually portions of a large cluster, and as such differ from the pot tubers or field tubers that you will receive from European tradesmen.

JAPAN

Yusaku Konishi (Dahlias), 455 Chibadera, Chibashi, Japan. Mr Konishi is the only Japanese dahlia nurseryman who speaks and writes English. His catalogues are in Japanese, of course, but important varieties have English names appended. Tubers travel well from the Orient, but can be expensive in terms of plant cost and postages (air mail).

Index

Soil Preparation 52
Soils 52
South Africa 103, 119, 121
Spain 9, 13
Specimen Dahlias 62, 64
Spent Hops 51, 59
Spotted Wilt 79, 80
Spraying 56, 69, 70
Stable and Farmyard Manures 51, 52, 59
Staggered Planting 107
Staging 11, 112
Stopping 59
Straw 56, 59, 95, 96, 97
'Stunt' Dahlia 79
Sulphur Dust, Flowers of 93
Summer Feeding 64, 108
Sybol 68
Symptomless Carriers 81, 82
Systemic Insecticide 71

Thiram 68

Thrips 67, 68, 71, 79
Trade Societies 81
Traps 73, 75
Trimming Tubers 90, 91, 95
Tuber Divisions 45, 47, 55
Tying 56, 60, 64

United States of America 27, 28, 37, 103, 116, 117, 118, 128, 129

Variabilis 13
Vermiculite 39, 95
Viruses 76, 77, 79, 80, 81

Wasps 67, 74, 75
Watering 56, 59
Water Lily Dahlias 24, 29, 120
Wilting 42
Winter Rot 92
Winter Storage 52, 75
Wireworms 67, 75, 84
Woodlice 67, 75